D0597280

Family Piles

Local agents run the livestock markets, hold antique
auctions, carry out structural surveys and play the
widow in the Christmas pantomine.

Nigel Colborn

Family Piles

With illustrations by
Nick Wright

CASSELL

Cassell Publishers Limited
Artillery House, Artillery Row
London SW1P 1RT

Copyright © Nigel Colborn 1990
Illustrations Copyright © Cassell 1990

First published 1990

British Library Cataloguing in Publication Data
Colborn, Nigel, *1944–*
   Family piles.
   1. Humour in English, 1945 – Texts
   I. Title
   828'.91409

ISBN 0–304–31802–7

Typeset by Input Typesetting Ltd, London

Printed and bound in Great Britain by Biddles Ltd., Guildford
and King's Lynn

For Rosamund

Enticed from her cosy Hampstead flat and now enslaved in a stone ruin, in the coldest part of Britain, miles from civilisation

Contents

Chapter 1

A Place in the Country

ALGERNON **Got nice neighbours in your part of Shropshire?**
JACK **Perfectly horrid! Never speak to one of them.**

(Oscar Wilde, *The Importance of Being Earnest*)

'In secluded, unspoilt English countryside,' says the agent's blurb. Immediately, you imagine grassy, rolling landscapes with flowery hedgerows and a tree-rich skyline. A herd of cattle might be grazing peacefully, while a cuckoo calls from the fragrant bluebell wood. 'Period cottage' you read, and into this arcadian dream you conjure up a half-timbered gem with roses round the windows and a thick crust of mellow thatch on top. This is the kind of con trick the countryside perpetrates. In reality, the cottage is probably a deathtrap, with mouldering roof and a garden full of uncharted, thirty-foot wells but no drainage – not even a septic tank. The cows will be out of sight, housed in an ugly asbestos building and fed by machines that dole out portions of silage with astonishing precision. The blue in the wood is not bluebells after all, but plastic fertiliser bags which hold rubbish dumped, illegally, by all and sundry.

In spite of the huge difference between the country image and reality, more people than ever before are forsaking urban bliss for what they see as a more wholesome life 'out there' in the shires.

Let's assume that you are determined to move out of town, regardless of grim warnings from friends who have tried it or from people already condemned, for various reasons, to a rustic existence. The first thing to remember is that country people fall into various categories. You will need to decide which category suits you best and, having once chosen, you must then learn how to lead an exemplary life in your chosen group. It is possible to transcend some of the barriers between categories but not all, and not often.

All aspects of rural life are dominated by ritual folklore. Authors and other literary souls warble on about the 'rhythm' of the countryside and 'nature' and the 'seasons' and all that. In fact, as you'll soon find out, the countryside, if it has a rhythm at all, is more like Schoenberg than Bach – unpredictable, difficult to understand and noisy. There are pitfalls and traps in all directions and the object of this book is to help guide you through the worst of them. You will need to know, for instance, how to pronounce the place names. Get them wrong and you'll elicit a torrent of scorn from the locals. The knack is to keep quiet until you hear the name from somebody else first. Just as a quick guide, here are one or two really tricky ones.

Spelling	Pronunciation
Ardingly	Arding lie
Aslackby	'azelby
Beaminster	Bempster
Beaulieu	Bewley
Berkhamsted	Bastard
Bosham	Bozzum (not Bosom and NEVER B'um)
Cholmondeley	Chumley (Bottomley, Bumley, etc.)
Chulmleigh	Cholmondeley
Cottesmore	Kotzmor (NEVER Kottiesmore)
Flushe Fytting	Fling
Godmanchester	God! Manchester (NEVER Gumpster)
Goodnestone	Gunston
Hautbois	Hobbis
Hunstanton	Hunston (Fenstanton = Fenstanton)

Ipswich	Ipswidge
Milton Keynes	Miles o' 'crete
Nantwich	Nantwitch, ha ha, gotcha!
Norwich	Norridge
St Neots	Snits
Shipbourne	Shibbun
Spalding	Sporlding (Lincolnshire: Spal-din)
Warminster	Whamster
Woolfardisworthy	Woolsery
Wormegay	Worm Eggy
Wymondham	Windum (Norfolk)
Wymondham	Why mond 'am (Leicestershire)
Yetts o'Muckhart	Y'tts o'M'ck'rrrt the noo, Jimmy!
Ysgubor-y-coed	um . . . er habla yd Inglese?

Before we get into more detail about your actual move, we should glance at the choices of county open to you. Many people believe that 'Rural Britain' means anywhere that isn't London, Manchester or Birmingham. This is a great illusion. The nation is set thick with cities, towns and conurbations, linked by motorways, all of which use up a shatteringly large proportion of our open spaces. Add uninhabitable areas like the moors, the fells, the Fens and most of Scotland, and you will see that the choice is more limited than you thought. Here is a mini-gazetteer to show you some places to aim for and others to avoid.

Undesirable

London Suburbs These include the whole of Kent, Surrey, Essex, Hertfordshire, Buckinghamshire, Berkshire, three-quarters of Sussex and half of Hampshire. Furthermore, where main railway lines run, suburbia continues 100 or more miles out of London. Peterborough, for example, is a London suburb. So are Oxford, Cambridge and Bath. It's hard to decide whether Bristol is a London suburb or part of Birmingham.

Big Conurbations These are the antithesis of rurality. They stretch for miles. Manchester, for example, runs from Blackpool on the west coast to Hartlepool on the east. Leeds, Bradford, Pontefract – not a cake to be seen there these days – Hull and Warrington are all parts of the great, grim, Northern Conurbation. There are a number of little rural pockets, like the Yorkshire Dales, the Trough of Boland and the North York Moors, but very few parts of these are fit for human habitation.

The Midlands Urban Sprawl runs from Birmingham down to Gloucester and across as far east as Leicester, engulfing Nottingham and Derby on its way.

East Anglia gets off lightly, having only Norwich, Ipswich, Essex, Cambridge and King's Lynn. The penalty is that, apart from half a mile on the Swaffham Bypass, there is no dual carriageway in Norfolk. That's why so many people retire there – they go there to visit but never have the courage to make the journey back again to the outside world.

The Desirable Shires

Devonshire Wonderful people, the Devonians. However, they became extinct long ago, hence the geological term 'Devonian Period'. Most of the county is spoilt by the M5, which disgorges West Midlanders into the leafy valleys at a rate of a million a day. Good gardening – plenty of rain. Dramatic gales in winter but pleasant topography apart from the coastline, which consists either of 1,000-foot cliffs or a sea of mud at low tide. Interesting wildlife, especially local stag hunters, who, having wiped out the red deer, now track down and eat tourists.

Languages: Cockney, Brum, some UCD (Upper-Class Drawl) in Tavistock. Devonian – for example, *'Noomye, lookit thacky ackymal, 'tes n'm'rna scriddick of a bird t'eat 'grt maskall'* ('Goodness, fancy a tiny blue tit managing to eat such a large caterpillar') – has died with its people.

Somerset An excellent county, full of the *right* sort of people.

Lots of genuine countryside, soft climate, many good gardens. Dreadful cyder and quite a lot of unemployment. Many tourists in summer so coastal dwelling is out of the question. One railway station, at Taunton, which is a London suburb.

Dorset Populated with Thomas Hardy lookalikes. Unless you intend to write a series of serious nineteenth-century novels with sombre plots and immaculate rural descriptions, don't choose the inland areas. Egdon Heath is now a wheat prairie, which Fowles things up for second-rate writers who rely on Hardy imitations for a living. Plenty of old fossils at Lyme Regis, where retired Indian Army officers live.

Wiltshire Wiltshire is an army camp with one excellent pub.

Gloucestershire Suitable for members of the Royal Family and horses. The Cotswolds are not fit for rural living because the villages are inhabited only at week ends. Other parts of the county are pleasantly rural.

Norfolk and Suffolk Excellent birdwatching. There is a constant east wind which makes you think the ice age is still running but the inland areas are wonderfully free of people and not everywhere is flat. Areas to avoid: Constable country, because hotel prices are so high and English-speaking people so rare (most visitors are Americans); the Norfolk Broads – a boat marina and ice-cream parlour covering a couple of hundred square miles on the county borders. The north Norfolk coast becomes invaded with twitchers and amateur mariners all summer. Conversations include alarming words like spinnaker, shrouds, burgees, pratincoles and merchant banks.

Lincolnshire If you thought Norfolk was cold you ain't felt nothin'. The flat bits of Lincolnshire are awful, but there are plenty of hills to the north and west and very few people. Pork butchery is the chief local industry and many inhabitants, despite outward appearances of excruciating poverty, have riches beyond the wildest dreams of avarice. Shooting is popular, so October is a month to avoid there unless you know what you are doing or want to end it all. The coast is horrible and Skegness as beastly as its name suggests.

Scotland Good scenery, plenty of fishing and golf. Too cold to garden except on the West Coast and a hell of a long way from London.

The Undesirable Shires

Cornwall Unlike Devonians, there is still a hardcore of native Corns. They are hostile to foreigners, but delight in parting them from their money. There is no town or country planning in Cornwall, where coastal villages have become vast shanty towns of beach stores, holiday homes and small hotels which change hands every year. From the Corns' point of view, they see their Duchy as having been completely ruined by tourists. They are quite right.

Hereford, Worcester and Shropshire This is a garden centre and nursery with a couple of moderate cathedrals – birthplace of Sir Ted Edgar, the enigmatic composer who started three-day events for choirs. Shropshire is where A. E. Housman, yearning for a Shropshire lad, fell to his death off Wenlock Edge in 1924. There's a thing called the Wrekin, possibly a kind of cottage loaf.

Yorkshire Too cold. People too blunt – well, let's face it, bloody rude.

Lancashire Too urban. Too wet.

Lakelandshire Fit only for romantic poets. Too crowded in summer, under an icecap in winter. Sellafield.

Walesshire Language problems. Poor train service. Too many disaffected miners. Good for musical types and Labour MPs. One or two fine gardens.

Well, there you are. Now you've been able to study the options open to you. Your next task is to look carefully at all the possibilities and then choose your rural area. Just bear in mind that price does not always reflect desirability – but it usually does. You must decide whether you want to be near the sea, meaning wind and summer tourists, or deep inland, meaning frost and intensive agriculture. Sparsely populated areas will have no services; crowded areas will be less rural and more expensive. The east is cold; the west is wet. You pays your money – lots and lots of it – and you takes your choice – very little of that.

As far as people are concerned, the first thing to bear in mind is that the country has a *structured* society. When you decide to take up life there, you will need to have a full understanding of its denizens. Money – how much or how little you have – will go some way towards deciding which slot you will fit into, but other factors are equally important. Your profession, your accent, the colour of your blood, your race and religion will also signify. To help you decide what to aim for, here are some family portraits. Let's start at the top – status-wise that is, not necessarily money-wise.

The Upper Crust

Everyone thinks the aristocracy are incredibly rich. Sometimes they are, but more often they are losing their marbles – both real and figurative – at a frightening rate. They struggle to keep their estates going, reduced to semi-starvation and living in a small back room of the stable block while 100,000 visitors a year admire their Gainsboroughs and wander through the William Kent landscapes. Their tragedy is that as soon as they have got their finances on to a more or less even keel, the wrong relative dies first, leaving horrific capital tax liabilities and blowing all the family financial strategy out of the window. To correct this problem, another Leonardo manuscript gets flogged or the family opens a funfair in the Italian Garden.

Yet despite their difficulties, these unfortunate souls are

expected to be unpaid guardians of the arts. To the man in the Clapham semi, the print of Constable's *Haywain* or the fishing gnome by his garden pool is his property, to do with as he likes. If he wants to dispose of them to make room for a flight of pot ducks, he can. However, the general public is never more indignant than when a duke threatens to double glaze his Tudor hall or to lay wall-to-wall carpeting in his rococo drawing room. 'Vandals,' cry the critics, from the comfort of their Kensington flats, 'Shameful,' moralises the *Sun*. 'Hands Off Our Heritage!' If the same duke peddles a picture to finance the modernizations, his name is mud.

Identifying the species

At village or country functions, look carefully for the blokes wearing green wellies and cow-dung-coloured jackets which look slept in. These are NOT aristocratic types. They are more probably estate agents trying to look rural or television producers who think they've gone native. Members of the Royal Family may, from time to time, don this kind of attire, but only for photo-opportunities. Likewise, arrogant-looking men and women who gallop past on well-groomed horses are more likely to be retired pork pie manufacturers than gentry. Your true aristo will be an unassuming little body who will scuttle forward to snip the ribbon on a new stretch of motorway, make a short, inaudible speech and rush back into the woodwork. Those who lead active lives in the House of Lords – where 'active' means they snore more loudly and twitch in their sleep – adopt an even lower profile. They seldom show much emotion about anything, because all that nonsense was thrashed out of them on the playing fields of Eton and their heart belongs to Nanny.

If you want to be an aristocratic type, you will have to be astronomically rich to be able to buy your way in. You don't have to belong to an old family but there should be a title on the way at some stage. Thanks to the hilariously antiquated ideas of the Conservative governments of the eighties, heritable titles are being dished out like sweeties at a kids' party. All you need do is be a civil servant, stand for parliament or develop a profitable business which makes handsome contributions to Party funds and your elevation to the peerage is comfortably assured. Getting titled is one of the few achievements where women are not at a serious disadvantage. If you are female and want a handle, all you need do is marry it. What could be simpler? You don't even need to stay married – you can still call yourself Lady Soandso and remain fragrant even after dumping your spouse.

A typical family

Fytting Hall, Flushe Fytting, is the seat of Lord Lagging. The house, set in 25,000 acres, was completed in 1602 by the Polish architect Vittorio di Ritornello. The seventeenth-century parterre remains intact, but the rest of the gardens were ripped out by the landscaper Humprey Brown-Repton (nicknamed Incapable Humph) in 1779 and replaced with a three-day eventing course, boating lake and rhododendron forest.

Lord Lagging's son, Dominic, is longing to inherit the title but doesn't want anything to do with the family pile. He lives in Kensington and is an expert on English watercolours. Being an art expert meant a long and rigorous education for Dominic. He didn't manage any 'O' levels but went straight to Rookham Fine Arts, somewhere in St James's, from his public school. The training took a whole month – managing to hold a picture up to the light and keep three plums in his mouth while he talked at the same time was the worst bit – but the effort was worthwhile and now he can afford the payments on his £100,000 mortgage.

Education is *so* important. Dominic will have cost his parents a fortune in school fees. At eight he was shipped off to shiver miserably in an underheated prep school, housed in some ancient rural pile last used by Oliver Cromwell to imprison royalists. Thence, having developed a keen understanding of playing the game, not being a sneak, cold showers, schoolboy crushes – either on Matron or the Captain of Cricket – he took the Common Entrance Exam and moved up to one of our great public schools. This was where he learned to accept his station in life as a naturally superior person and where he made all the contacts necessary for a successful future career. Since university was out of the question – in fact, let's face it, Dominic was about as keen on academia as Attila the Hun was on liberalism – there was not a very wide

choice of career open to him. No Oxbridge, so there were no
openings in the KGB. Medicine was out, the Law was too boring
and even land agents have to pass exams. No, there was nothing
for it but to join one of the London art auctioneers. There, in the
company of effete youths and horsy gels, he soon developed the
knack of sorting out the fakes from the genuine articles. Most of
his work is done during a social whirl of parties:

'Fiona!'

'Dominic! Fancy seeing you hyar!'

'Likewise. I didn't know you were working for Christeby's!'

'Oh yah! I've bin there for nearly a month. Antiques!'

'Well, yah. Wouldn't expect much else at Christeby's!'

'Nair. I mean hyar, at this *dreadful* parterre.'

'Parterre? This is a terrace.'

'Near, silly, p-a-r-t-e-y parterre!'

'Ear. Ear, I see. You mean antique *people*! Ear, how terriblea
funnea. Mind you, you must be learning an awful lot at Christeby's. I know I am at Rookham Fine Arts.'

'Ear years. One soon finds ite how to spot the genuine article.
I mean, take this thing here, for instance. Clearly bogus.'

'How can you tell?'

'Wrong lustre on the black surface for a start. The globes are
far too small. Besides, it just doesn't have the texture.'

'Near, well, they probably couldn't afford real caviar.'

'Near, I don't suppose they could. Anyway, lumpfish roe treads
into the carpet just as well, yah?'

'Ear, Fiona, you are an absolute scream. You really ought –
Oh, damn, I've sloshed champagne over my clothes. Real champagne too, for once. What a waste, still –'

'Dominic, quick! Get your trisers off!'

'Sorry? Ear, near problem. It won't stain, it's Dom Perignon.'

'No, you idiot! Get your trisers off anyway, quickly, the *Tatler*
photographer's coming this way!'

That's probably enough to give you a taste of the aristocratic
life.

Fast-Track Professionals

Successful professionals are one step down from the gentry. Some may be linked with the aristocracy but they are all at the top of their professions – brain surgeons, QCs, MPs and marketing consultants. They tend to live in substantial period houses, where opulence is evident without being too ostentatious. Traditionally, the wives of SPs would be pillars of the establishment, organising Meals on Wheels, chairing parish councils and running endless coffee mornings to raise funds for the vicar's organ. Nowadays, many of them are successful professionals themselves and prefer to gad about in adapted men's suits, running public companies or starting chains of boutiques selling *haute couture* items they wouldn't be seen dead in themselves to wealthy females who wouldn't be seen dead in adapted men's suits. The SP has to commute to the city every day. He leaves home at six-thirty every morning and returns after nine at night, so he only sees the garden in daylight on the odd weekend when they decide to stay at home instead of going to their croft in the North-West Highlands of Scotland.

You probably know plenty of SPs yourself. Have you met James Pricey-Breaf, QC, of Flushe Manor, the second biggest house in Flushe Fytting? No? Well, you will have to get to know him if you're intending to move into this area. Their house was completed in 1780 – lovely mellow brickwork and rounded walls with pretty classical portico. James and Lavinia moved in three years ago. They paid over the odds, but you should have seen the place before they came. Belonged to a mink farmer who kept the animals in some of the rooms. Ugh! They arrived one Monday with a retinue of architects, woodworm specialists, builders, landscape designers and other 'experts'. The builders put their little sign on the front gate and then disappeared for three months. Then, quite suddenly, it all started. A crane arrived and bashed off the chimney stacks. The sound of pneumatic drills reverberated through the village all summer, while crews of building workers arrived each morning, made tea, worked for an hour, made coffee, worked for another hour, went home to lunch, came back, made tea, worked for a third hour and then packed up for the day. From time to time, neat little men in dark suits appeared on the premises with clipboards in their hands and plastic helmets on their heads. Usually, after they'd gone, a bit of new wall or a freshly installed window frame was removed and rebuilt.

Eventually, months behind schedule, the renovations were completed. Inside, it looks exactly the same as it did before, except that all the pests have been eliminated and faulty structures put right. The owners are £100,000 poorer, but their lovely period gem is sound – for the present.

In his spare time – his what? – James enjoys dry fly fishing. Lavinia hates his fishing tackle in the house but they are going to convert the stable into a hobbies room so that she can do her upholstery and he his fly tying without spoiling the decor of the manor house. The idea came to them during a discussion – well, a row really – about Lavinia's career.

'I want to start a business,' she had said one day and then amended herself, 'I am going to start a business.'

'Splendid, darling,' murmured James from the depths of the *Angling Times*.

'I'll have finished my upholstery classes next month and want to get to grips with it. Beryl Weinstein says we should form a partnership.'

'Splendid.'

'James, you are listening, aren't you?'

'Splendid.'

'I'll need capital – plenty.'

'Beryl Weinstein's got plenty.'

'Really? I thought you said Sol was on the brink of destitution?'

'Plenty of upholstery, I mean. Talk about top-heavy.'

'Don't be disgusting. How much can we afford?'

'We?' He had lost interest in the *Angling Times* by now. 'We?'

'Mm. I'll need a workshop. Beryl will do the customer relations bit – they're all such worms – while I get stuck into the hammering and bashing. Then there's tools and things – a van, typewriters, a computer, I should think – and, of course, we'll need a pretty big stock of materials.'

'Are you perfectly serious? I mean, do you realise what you are saying?'

'I think so. Beryl and I want to start an upholstery business. I'll be calling on some of our *joint* capital.'

'Oh?' He's really losing his rag by now. 'And what sort of capital would that be?'

'Well, you know, we could sell some shares or something.'

'Dear God! Don't you remember the stock-market crash? We cannot, cannot, cannot sell anything. The repairs to this hell hole of a manor cost thirty thou more than we budgeted for, Jeremy is spending his university grant four times over, Fiona has married a twit who can't stay sober long enough to fill in a job application form, you insist on a gardener who charges me fifty quid to kill the plants and nurture the weeds for two mornings a week, our mortgage is topped up to the hilt and you ask me for capital?'

'Oh, well, if you're going to be negative. Just because you object to me having a mind of my own.'

'Besides, Beryl's dodgy. She made a complete balls-up of that boutique.'

'Right. If you're going to be an obstructive pig, you can get your bloody fishing rods the hell out of my morning room.'

'It is not your morning room. It's *my* study.'

'Just get them out. And that creel thing. It really stinks.'

'And where am I supposed to put them?'

'Shove 'em where they belong.'

'There's no need for coarseness.'

'Put them in the stable. That's where messy hobbies should go.'

'Messy hobbies? Like upholstery – hey! There's an idea. The stable.'

'The stable? The stable! Darling! You clever old thing. We could tart it up ever so cheaply.'

'True.'

'It'd improve the value of the house too.'

'True.'

'You always said this place was our main asset.'

'Also true.'

'So, why don't we do the stable up properly to make a decent workshop there? You could have a special room for twiddling with your flies.'

'Tying.'

'And now I don't need to buy a shop. We could do up the top
floor as well. Make a home for poor dear mother.'

'Do what?'

The Nouveau Owner

These days, many of the better country houses are being taken
over by people who have become wealthy quite quickly, in spite
of socially deprived backgrounds. The Old Rectory at Flushe
Fytting is a good example. Matt Vinyl lives there with his current
common-law wife, Magnolia. You must have heard of Matt.
Everyone has. He grew up in Wapping, survived an inner-city
comprehensive and left school at sixteen to train as a motor
mechanic. He now has a substantial business empire, two ex-
wives, a collection of assorted children and a Gauguin. When they
moved in, they toured the house with the same retinue of experts
as the Pricey-Breafs. The big difference was that Matt owns the
building company. The men used to arrive at seven and work
through to five every day. Sometimes they even worked through
their lunch hours.

Of course, Matt has some pretty radical ideas about housing
design. The essence of his plan was to create a Beverly Hills Late
Wedding Cake Mansion bang in the middle of Flushe Fytting. He
says he loves the quiet charm of the English village. The Old
Rectory was early nineteenth century but he reckoned it made a
perfect basis for the project. Listed? No, he said it wasn't listed.
He couldn't understand why not. Couldn't believe his luck when
he found out. You should see the inside. He built an American-
style Pool Hall in the old drawing room, a sauna and Jacuzzi in
the butler's pantry and set his nine-foot double bed on a stage
surrounded by revolving mirrors. All that without any form of
let or hindrance from any of the planning authorities. Everyone
wonders how on earth he gets away with it all but are too scared
to ask. They say he gives very strange parties. But then, you know
what villagers are like, don't you? If you don't, you soon will.

Cottagers Ancient and Modern

Obviously, most villages contain no more than a couple of fine houses. There is usually a rectory or vicarage, a farmhouse or two, perhaps a manor house or a dower house, but most of the dwellings are smaller and less pretentious. Period cottages often share the street with gems of the 1930s and post-war council houses. Inhabitants of these lesser abodes fall into two main categories – natives and foreigners. A foreigner is anyone born more than five miles away from the village centre, and of this despised group the worst of all are the weekenders. In some areas, the Cotswolds for example, there are no original resident cottagers left in any of the villages. They have all moved away to make room for foreigners and weekenders. A short conversation with a resident cottager leaves you in no doubt about how local opinion runs as far as outsiders are concerned.

Farmers

Until the seventies farmers were the salt of the earth. Thanks to their noble efforts, a grateful post-war nation was fed with good, healthy things like eggs, bacon, beef and lamb. Cream was a luxury which apple-cheeked farmers' wives would ladle into proffered jars or jugs for a shilling or so. Over the years, technology enabled them to produce these foodstuffs ever more abundantly and the era of austerity and rationing soon faded into the dusty corners of old memories.

Nowadays, farmers are destructive swine who are wrecking the countryside and poisoning everybody with evil chemicals. Eggs, bacon, beef and lamb are so unhealthy for life in the nineties that some people think livestock should be tattooed at birth with government warnings. Persons buying eggs should sign the poisons book and, as for cream, it would be safer to swallow weedkiller than to risk all that deadly cholesterol. To add to their evil natures, farmers also receive mammoth subsidies from the

Nowadays, farmers are destructive swine who are
wrecking the countryside and poisoning everybody
with evil chemicals.

Common Market. When he wants to change his Rolls-Royce or BMW, all the farmer has to do is fill in a form and the new vehicle is delivered at once. He gets paid handsomely for growing wheat but he also gets paid handsomely for not growing wheat. In farming it's a 'no lose' situation for everyone. And, as if all that were not enough, because of their evil, greedy ways, farmers have produced huge mountains of unwanted things like butter, beef and grains.

How did farmers change from saintly providers of sustenance to arch villeins? (It's a pun, not a spelling mistake – my jokes are positively *feudal*!) The answer is simple. They got their *public image* altered. In reality, they're no different from the rest of us and, though techniques have changed, the job they do is the same now as it was in the fifties. Furthermore, they have to live with the idiotic rules and regulations designed by the Common Market. These have to be studied to be believed:

'Hullo. Have you any fresh cream?'

'Yes.'

'May we buy some?'

'No. We aren't allowed to sell it to you.'

'Why not?'

'Because we have to sell all our milk to the Milk Marketing Board. We're not licensed to sell to the likes of you.'

'Why's that?'

'Don't ask me, Sunshine. I don't make the rules, I just live by them.'

'But how ridiculous. I thought the EEC had a dairy surplus.'

'It does.'

'So why can't you let us have a little of your surplus?'

'Against regulations. You could go to Abbey Farm, just down the lane. They could sell it to you.'

'Illegally?'

'No, no. Perfectly legit.'

'I'm sorry. I don't quite follow.'

'Unpasteurised. Has his own milk round. Makes his own cheese too. In fact, he can't produce enough to satisfy his customers' needs.'

'Can he buy extra milk to make more farmhouse cheese?'

'Not legally, except pasteurised stuff from the MMB.'

'Well, what's wrong with that?'

'People only buy his cheeses *because* they're made from unpasteurised milk. He reckons he could sell twice as much as he does now. He even has shops in London wanting his produce.'

'So he could help to erode the surplus by clever marketing but regulations won't let him have any more raw materials?'

'You've got it!'

In spite of their awful press, farmers are still widely respected in rural circles, and furthermore, they tend to own most of the land around the villages. Often, they are the only truly indigenous residents in the area.

Young Perspirers

These are energetic souls who have grown tired of their converted warehouse flats in the docks and yearn for a rural life. They are always well off and usually pretty shrewd when it comes to investing their own money, even if they are far too free and easy with other people's. They adore living in eccentric environments and do conversion jobs on Wesleyan chapels, barns, police stations, railway signal boxes and, in one case, a gents' lavatory – conveniently located, no doubt. Most conversions prove to be costly and difficult, but this is meat and drink to young perspirers, because they *love* a challenge.

Well, there you are. By now you should have a pretty good idea of where you are likely to fit in the rural hierarchy. Just to make sure you have grasped the significant points, here are some exercises. If you can answer all the questions correctly, move on to Chapter 2. If not, go on anyway. You might get better as you go along.

1 Whose stately pile was too, too divine and Gött burnt down?
(a) Valhalla, (b) 22 Railway Cuttings, East Cheam,
(c) Uffington Hall, (d) Mr Polly's shop.

2 Where in the UK could you expect the the warmest welcome?
(a) Wales, **(b)** Cornwall, **(c)** Scapa Flow, **(d)** Peterborough Station.

3 Where is the true Rural Heart of the country?
(a) A Scottish grouse muir, **(b)** the Somerset levels, **(c)** the Isle of Axholme.

4 How would you solve the problems of the Common Agricultural Policy?
(a) By updating combine harvesters, **(b)** by returning to traditional farming techniques, **(c)** by appointing a marketing expert, **(d)** by abolishing the House of Lords.

Answers

1 Manderley. Half a point if you got any of the others except for **(b)**, which was not really a stately pile.

2 The Swiss Centre, Leicester Square.

3 The Farmers' Club, Whitehall.

4 By starting another Hundred Years War with France. (Answers **(a)**, **(b)** and **(c)** are the prime *causes* of the CAP's problems.)

Chapter 2

Introducing the Professionals

The greatest trust between man and man is the trust of giving counsel.

(Francis Bacon, *Essay on Counsel*, 1625)

If you want to buy a Rolls-Royce, all you have to do is walk into a garage, choose your model and await delivery. When it arrives you just write a cheque for the odd £60,000 and drive it out of the garage, hoping it will get you home before its first breakdown. But if you want to buy a house, even a shack costing less than the Rolls, you need professional advice. Buying any rural dwelling, from a modern bungalow to a fifteenth-century manor, is a dangerous and exasperating exercise. Every set of deeds bristles with potential pitfalls. There are ancient grazing rights, riparian rights, covenants to supply the whole village with fuel on Michaelmas Day, neighbours' licences to abstract water from the well under your larder floor, easements, wayleaves and so on. Legal help will be essential and you should not wince too much when you get your solicitor's bill after completion, even though it's double the amount you expected.

Besides solicitors, you'll need counsel from a whole bevy of professional advisers. Don't think for one instant that I'm under-estimating your experience in these matters, but have you yet suffered the peculiar set of professionals who take care of *rural* transactions? Rustic professionals move at the pace of a Russian novel and have not yet discovered telephones, let alone Fax machines. Country architects are often escapees from the urban rat race, hiding out after one of their inner-city tower blocks of flats collapsed. The aim of this chapter is to acquaint you with the sleepy characters whose job it is to make your move to the country as traumatic and expensive as possible.

Estate Agents

Estate agents are not just there to sell properties. They do a great many other things, but most of their pay comes from commission on property sales. Most people wish they could sell their houses without an agent. Some even try, but to avoid coming unstuck, it's better to play safe, pay through the nose and retain an agent. You may feel the same way about buying and decide to use an agent to acquire your country house. 'Set a thief to catch a thief', don't they say?

Estate agents are masters of fiction. Their literary skills enable them to be capable of hyperbole and euphemism at the same time. In agents' language a delapidated *fin-de-siècle* ruin on the outskirts of Leicester becomes: 'In the heart of Quorn country. An important period mansion of great beauty, with scope for modernization'. Think how often, when you are house hunting, the particulars of that perfect dream home arrive in the post. It is not until you have actually dialled the agent's number for an appointment to view that you realise the particulars in your hand are of your own house.

When reading particulars, just remember that the hyperbole comes in equal proportion to the euphemism. Take a typical piece of agent's fiction:

One hour from King's Cross. Unique opportunity to purchase, in quiet, unspoilt countryside, a fine gentleman's sporting estate comprising the magnificent Georgian residence, *circa* 1800 (sympathetically modernised to the highest standards), set in thirty acres of productive land (MAFF Grade 4) with extensive woodland and bisected by the River Scriddicke, offering nearly a mile of trout and salmon fishing. Most of the sporting rights available.

Which, being interpreted, means:

Too near London to be really rural. A farmhouse, completed in 1884, is available with a few acres. It was wired for electricity and piped for mains water in 1957 but these services have not been altered or checked since then.

Too small to use as a realistic shoot (real gentlemen's estates would be nearer 30,000 acres) and too small to run as a viable farm. Local folklore has it that a single trout was once spotted in the Scriddicke, but this is unlikely since a two-year-old could, without undue exertion, step over the widest point of the river. The vendor is keeping all the shooting rights except over a small paddock and between the cluster of corrugated tin sheds and asbestos buildings which surround the house. There are a few trees on the southern edge of the property, which is just as well because they hide the development going on between the neighbouring fields and the M1.

Country estate agents fall into two categories. The big national firms have head offices in the smartest parts of London's West End. The partners all have Volvo estate cars or Range Rovers and wear green wellingtons, tweed caps and mangled shooting jackets. In the backs of their Volvos you will find all the necessary agents' equipment: shot gun, half a Stilton, shooting gloves and cartridges, auger for soil testing, rabbiting spade, golf (pronounced go'f) clubs, fishing rods, creel, waterproof trousers and Labrador. Big national agents have branch offices in all the important country towns. They are expert at all country activities, including fishing, farming, shooting, hunting, adultery and hare coursing.

When a young lad (women are expressly forbidden) who wants to be a big national agent leaves his public school he usually goes straight into a firm as a pupil. He then spends a year or two tailing one of the senior partners, learning to develop his vowel sounds and to win the right sort of shooting invitations. As he progresses, there are exams to pass, and these can be tricky because they involve awkward things like measuring buildings and counting hay bales. Assuming he is able to pass, he then serves time at a series of market town branches, until one fine day he is invited to work at head office.

In contrast, local country agents are fixed to one spot. Besides selling farms and houses, your local agent will also run the live-stock market, hold antique auctions, carry out structural surveys and play the Widow in the Christmas pantomime.

Local land agents must not be confused with house agents, whom they despise. The main difference between land agents and house agents is that the latter often cut their commissions to attract more business. They can do this because they haven't always passed the necessary exams to join the Institute of Chartered Surveyors and do not, therefore, belong to the cartel. Besides, most of them have been to grammar school or worse!

By using their own special language, all professionals make the simplest functions sound complicated. To overcome this problem, a glossary will appear at various points in this chapter to help you understand what is being said when people try to pull the wool over your eyes.

Augur An official of ancient Rome who presided over feasting and bouts of sexual excess. Auguring was an essential part of the aspiring Roman estate agent's training – see Virgil's *Aenioldiron* Book 2, lines 32–36. Translated:

> Young Marcus hath a mega bash laid on
> And all our friends tonight will have much fun
> Which augurs well for this young organiser
> Who hopes to be my father's agent's partner.

Deposit 1. An ancient custom of paying 10 per cent of the value of the purchase in the hopes that the vendors will consider a deal to have been struck. Has come to mean: a bit of free money while the vendor awaits a better offer. 2. Material left on the side of the bath in hard-water areas.

Firm Opposite to tender.

Gazumping The action of hurling objects, especially telephones, to the ground, after being told that a house vendor (qv) has reneged on a deal and accepted a higher offer from someone else.

Housing chain Chain to hold houses together. Widely used in hurricane zones.

Leasehold Having the full burden of responsibility for a property without actually owning it. You also pay rent and at the end of the alloted period the house is snatched back.

Particulars Exceptionally dense fogs which afflicted London in the late 1800s. Now only seen in horror films and Chinese restaurants (*see* Peasouper).

Peasouper Cockney rhyming slang for someone who hangs about spying on other people (cf. Barnet, Hampstead, Jimmy O' Goblin, plates, etc).

Private treaty A bribe. If, when trying to secure planning approval, your land agent slips the chief planning officer a case of champagne, this is known as a private treaty. For smaller concessions, a box of chocolates might suffice – this would be called a sweety treaty.

Purchaser The buyer of your home – subject to contract, survey, present home getting sold (*see* Housing chain), wife not changing mind, daughter not deciding to marry and emigrate to Australia, sound finances, building society approval and a fat slice of good luck besides.

Sale by auction Potential buyers prepare to bid while the auctioneer calls a continual increase in price based on imaginary bids from the back of the room. Eventually one of two things happen: (a) the reserve price is not reached and everything peters out. Later a little man in builders' overalls in the corridor outside turns out to have bought the property for half the reserve price after the auction is finished (*see* Private treaty); (b) the reserve price is exceeded by a factor of three, the vendor faints and the purchaser is frogmarched up to the table to sign the contract and write a deposit cheque, which he hopes to goodness won't be presented before he has had time to ring his bank manager and explain why it is four times the maximum figure they had agreed.

Signboard A board composed of civil servants and elected representatives who decide on the design and positioning of estate agents' 'for sale' notices, ensuring maximum visual obstruction to motorists.

Sold – subject to contract Not sold at all.

Structural survey Exercise in which a surveyor (qv) arrives at the house, tears the carpet, peels bits of wallpaper off and pulls plug wires out. He then makes a report on how the fittings are damaged.

Tender Soft, pliable, easily chewed – applies to clients.

Vendor Part of a commercial vehicle invariably opened into oncoming traffic.

Apart from the need to understand estate agents' technical jargon, you must also have a thorough knowledge of their 'adspeak'. No doubt you are already familiar with their romanticisation of urban properties eg: 'Ample Parking' when the photograph above shows a double yellow and a bus stop in front of the house or, 'In the heart of fashionable Holland Park' when they really mean the rougher end of Shepherd's Bush or, 'West Hampstead' meaning Kilburn and so on, but how well do you read their rural adspeak? 'A charming period cottage with wisteria-clad elevations' sounds lovely until you realise that the wisteria is holding up the elevations. Here are some phrases to watch for:

Architect designed Everything in this house is one-off and untried. Roof leaks, windows don't fit, and the swimming pool in the attic was rather a mistake.

Charming Recently painted pink.

Close to local amenities Between the main London–Glasgow railway and the sewage works.

Deceptively spacious It's even smaller than you feared.

Desirable Undesirable.

Distinctive A blot on the landscape.

Executive home Hideous, over-priced modern outrage built of the wrong materials in the wrong place. Most of the garden space will be taken up with a double garage whose doors are skillfully painted with the back ends of a Mercedes and a BMW.

Full of character Ugly.

Gardens
1 Large plot = less than 1/10th acre of builder's rubble.
2 Large garden = less than 1/10th acre of bare soil.

3 Extensive gardens = more than 1/10th acre but less than 1/4 acre.

4 Extensive mature gardens = 1/10th acre of lawn with a shrub in it.

5 Secluded walled garden = a small area of ill-lit ground surrounded by high buildings

Hamlet No shop, no church, no post office, no bus, no pub, nobody.

Idyllic setting Overlooking a wide river which is infested with lagerlouts every summer and floods the cellar every winter.

Important Unimportant but expensive.

Imposing Large, arrogant and designed to attract burglars.

Imaginatively restored Recently painted purple.

In immaculate order Recently painted white.

In the heart of –

1 The Lakesmoor National Park = swarming with tourists from March to November.

2 Fitzbeauquorn hunting country = hunt saboteurs and mounted gentry will be slagging each other off in your front garden.

3 Thomas Hardy/Lorna Doone/The Brönte Sisters country = see 1 above.

4 D. H. Lawrence/Robin Hood/Charles Dickens country = grim suburbs or slums.

5 Graham Greene/Ernest Hemingway/Anthony Burgess country = doesn't mean anywhere, it's a state of mind.

Isolated Miles from the nearest road.

Modernisation

1 With scope for modernisation = about to fall down.

2 In need of modernisation = has already fallen down.

3 Sympathetically modernised = nothing has been done other than putting new wallpaper over the old damp patches.

4 Modernised to the highest specifications = wallpaper over damp patches and spotlights installed over the pictures.

5 Tastefully modernised = as 4 but coach lamps installed by the front door as well.

Listed grade 2 More than twenty years old. You won't be allowed to do anything to it.

Listed grade 1 You won't even be allowed to stand a ladder against it without risking a heavy fine.

Offers in excess of X 'X' = 3 times the maximum price expected.

Outstanding A blot on the landscape.

Part central heating Someone left a disconnected radiator leaning against the guest room wall.

Price on Application Not really for sale, the owners just want to find out what the place is worth.

Much sought after You'll never find it.

Picturesque Collapsing (with estate agents in mind, perhaps it should be 'picaresque').

Quaint Collapsed.

Quiet residential area In a town.

Rarely available Hardly ever off the market because purchasers find it's impossible to live in.

Retaining many original features Like rising damp, dry rot and a charnel house odour.

Secluded Not semi-detached.

Set in water meadows It floods.

Split level House and garden both slope at an angle of 45°.

Superbly presented Recently painted white.

Unique One of six identical houses, each with a different coloured front door.

Within walking distance of Up to five miles from.

Solicitors

Most country solicitors have offices in the market square, usually up a set of rickety stairs over the hairdresser's or next door to the dentist. In these offices, you'll find a great deal of mahogany and dust. There will be glass-fronted bookcases containing ancient legal tomes and an antique wooden filing cabinet on which sits a decanter and sherry glasses. The desk will be a grand affair with tooled-leather top. Your lawyer, a Mr Fuddle of Tweed, Fuddle and Grope, will be sitting behind it, bolt upright, in an all-wooden chair which looks as if it was designed to induce lumbago. He will be extraordinarily wrinkled, looking about ninety-five and almost too frail to support the weight of his heavy tweed jacket. You are shown to the only other chair in the room by a decrepit secretary, who then returns to her small cave behind the filing cabinet, where she resumes her losing battle with the 1948 Olivetti.

'I do apologise,' says the ancient man o' law. 'I'm afraid my father is not available today so you will have to make do with me.'

'Aren't you Mr Fuddle?'

'Fuddle junior. At your service.'

'Ah. Fine. I, er, plan to move into this district and wondered whether you would act for me. I, well, we have found the house we want.'

'Yes?'

'The old farmhouse in Mullions Whamstead. The one at the end of the green lane, by that lovely old wood.'

'Ah, yes, I know. Between the railway and the pylons. I'd heard the Rednecks were moving out but hadn't seen it advertised. Who are the agents?'

'Gluttons.'

'Local office or London?'

'Local.'

'Ah. Good. That's Fiennes Gorrington-Persse. Excellent feller. First-rate background. His father is Lord Bevelledge, you know.'

'No, I didn't know.'

'Oh yes. Splendid feller. Mind you, you'll have trouble with the Rednecks. They've something of a . . . '

'Reputation?'

'Bad name. Never pay their bills.'

'Well, I've made an offer, so perhaps I should ask you to draw up a contract.'

'Woah! Not so fast, young feller. Now, first things first. I ought to have an acceptance of your offer, in writing, from young Fiennes. We'll write to him this week.'

'Write?'

'Certainly, young feller. No hurry. No point in telephoning. Save the cost of a phone call.'

'But is that not Gluttons' office that I can see through your window, on the opposite side of the square?'

'Certainly.'

'Well, couldn't your secretary nip over with a note?'

'A note? Good heavens, you *are* in a hurry.'

'Well, it might save time.'

'No need, my dear feller. Now, let me give you a glass of sherry. You need not concern yourself for the present with the house.' At this point he seems to drift into a sort of Joycean reverie. 'Rum, those Rednecks, very rum. Wonder why they're moving out . . . rumours . . . wonder if it's true. They say the most unlikely people. Yes. Might she? Stable lad . . . Yes.' Suddenly, the ancient eyes click back into focus. 'Heavens, my dear feller. I'm so sorry, I was miles away. What was I saying?'

'The, ah, Rednecks.'

'Ah, to be sure. Still farming there, of course. Fed up with the trains perhaps. Now, let me see. There's the search, that will take about six weeks; then we ought to allow for some of that Redneck stubbornness. Renowned for it round here, they are. Still, I don't suppose you'll want to move in this side of Christmas, will you?'

'But today is only 9 August!'

'Really! As late as that? Ah, well, Christmas will be out of the question. But I suppose if we exert a little pressure from our end we could complete before next Easter. Would that suit you?'

'Well, if that's the fastest you –'

'Capital, capital. Now do have some sherry.'

When he lifts the decanter, a little swirl of sediment rises from the bottom and clouds the wine. He proffers the glass but does not pour himself one.

'What about you?'

'Me? At this hour? Good heavens, no. I have to keep an alert head on my shoulders. As you'll find out when you've had further dealings with the Rednecks.'

'Well, cheers!' you mutter. It tastes as foul as it looks but eventually you are able to unpucker the lips and say, 'I'll telephone later in the week to see how things are going.'

'No need, no need. Well, if it makes you feel better. By the way, there is one little point I should suggest.'

'Well?'

'I think you should make out a cheque for the deposit. Just in case we effect an exchange of contracts sooner than I expected. 10 per cent is the usual.'

'That's £24,000!'

'Twenty-four? Good gracious me. My dear young man, what *can* you have offered?'

'Less than they were asking.'

'Extraordinary! Still, perhaps you should just leave a cheque.'

Of course, the longer the old boy can stall the deal, the longer he can earn interest on the deposit money.

Legal language is even more confusing than agent's language. Much of it is in a kind of dog Latin or worse, arising from a single legal action that may have happened several centuries ago. Here is a small selection of difficult words which every rural house purchaser should understand.

Absolute title Unencumbered ownership. The Englishman's castle. Nobody can take it away from him – apart from HM Inspector of Taxes, Customs and Excise, the Department of the Environment, Ministry of Agriculture, Fisheries and Food, God and the Queen.

Advocate An alcoholic drink made of spirits and egg yolk and consumed by Dutch lawyers. (Not to be confused with advocaat – a pear shaped fruit with oily flesh.)

Affidavit A sworn statement. DIY enthusiasts often resort to affidavits when they hammer their thumbs.

Ancient lights The right of an outgoing householder to take all electrical fittings, including sockets, light bulbs, plugs and even fuse boxes, despite the sale having been stipulated as 'including fittings'.

Barrister A lawyer who thinks he (or she) can make enough of a living without having to do conveyancing, which is excessively lucrative but very boring. Disadvantages are having to wear hot, itchy wigs and other fancy dress items designed to frighten the life out of the criminal classes.

Called to the Bar Being offered a free drink – only happens to lawyers.

Ceteris paribus A passenger carrying vehicle designed to treat all classes equally.

Codicil A type of window ledge extension, usually nailed on as an afterthought.

Conveyance Any form of transport – car, aircraft, chariot, etc.

Deduced – as in 'Title shall be deduced and commence . . . ' A curious expression arising from the layman's total inability to understand a word of the contract he is about to sign.

Deed poll The post from which felons were hanged. Much in demand for supporting climbing roses these days, a genuine seventeenth-century deed poll can sell for thousands.

Easement Expansion of a gateway to allow access for wide vehicles.

Garnishee A person on whom notice is served that his money will be seized, legally, in the near future. Traditionally, the solicitor's clerk places a sprig of parsley on the garnishee's head before serving the writ.

Hereditament It, as in you can't take 'it' with you. What all the relatives fight over after your death. Without hereditaments, the Novel would not exist as an art form.

Pari passu Simultaneously – if your buyers don't sell their house *pari passu* they won't be able to pay for yours and you will lose the chance of buying, *pari passu*, your country home and your country home vendors (qv) won't be able, *pari passu*, to get their flat in Kilburn – sorry, West Hampstead – and the flat owners won't . . .

Quasi Nauseous.

Sic transit Moisture-proof receptable for use during spells of travel discomfort (*see* Quasi).

Silk – as in 'taking silk'. QCs take silk. Exactly what they do with it is either unclear or unhealthy, or both, but it is their silk that sets them apart from mere solicitors.

Solicitor A lawyer unable to afford silk, which is odd, considering the fees charged when you move house.

Statutory declaration A promise, made under oath, on the part of the vendor not to take garden ornaments and other outdoor structures with him when he moves out – gnomes are not usually included in this undertaking.

Tontine A sort of contest where the hereditament (qv) goes, by prior agreement, to the member of a group of beneficiaries who manages to live longest and who successfully evades a conviction for murder.

Zonk The action of placing a finger, toe or other portion of the anatomy on the red dot on a document before making a sworn declaration.

By the time you have purchased the house, you may think that your worst brushes with the professionals are nearly over – but that's reckoning without architects and builders.

Architects

Architects occupy that terrifying 'no go' area between art and science. A true artist's mind surges with lyrical inspiration, so that, on compulsion, he will spend the next decades painting indescribably beautiful things on a chapel cistern, say, or on the walls of Crookham Church. Although such masterworks have no functional purpose at all, their very beauty is what separates us from the animals. (After all, what animal admires scenes depicting acts of unspeakable violence being done to his fellow species?) Architects' heads are full of angles rather than angels and of worries about loading, stress and complying with building regulations. With all that on their minds, little space is left for aesthetics.

The death-blow to good twentieth-century architecture came when a certain Royal Personage began to criticise the new monstrosities. Mindful of losing out on possible OBEs, not to mention knighthoods, even the most avant-garde architects began to knock up depressing and uninspired imitations of Doric temples and other classical grot. So today, if you want a new public building, you have the choice of something that looks like a motorway pile-up or a windowless replica of an earlier replica of a Victorian replica of an Adam Palladian replica of a medieval replica of a Roman replica of a Greek temple, complete with Corinthian columns topped with acanthus leaves.

Luckily for you, the countryside is littered with genuine

eighteenth- and nineteenth-century replicas of earlier replicas of . . . etc. However, because the particular gem you are buying was probably last used to house turkeys and is suffering from structural decay, you'll need the services of a good architect to help you to obtain listed building consent for a 'sympathetic' renovation.

Because of all the maths filling their heads, architects are not always quick to catch on to what you are trying to say. They also have strange ideas about how people like to live, so you will need to know exactly what *you* want to do with your house. They are really only there to tell you which of your ideas add up to a practical proposition – the maths again – and then to take all the credit for your inspiration. Suppose you have just bought a derelict cottage with part-thatched roof and a single-storey wing at the back. You want to expand the accommodation from two poky bedrooms to four roomy ones, with at least one extra bathroom. Enter the architect, looking puzzled.

'What do you want this place for?' he asks.

'To live in.'

'You can't do that. It's condemned. Not fit for habitation.'

'We know. That's why we asked you to come and have a look at it.'

'Ah.'

'We have some ideas.'

'Oh?' He looks alarmed. 'Listed, is it?'

'Yes.'

'Bad luck! They've listed everything built before the Falklands Campaign in this part of the world, I'm afraid. My neighbour left her Morris Minor Estate parked in the village high street last year and the local authority listed it as "an important timber-frame structure".'

'But this cottage is grade two star. We thought that was rather good.'

'Makes things very difficult. You'll never get away with patio doors.'

'Patio doors? Perish the thought! These half-doors are original.'

'Ah.'

'We wanted to keep the old world charm at the front but at the back, where the dining room has no top floor, we thought we'd make an extra storey.'

'I'm sorry, I don't quite follow.'

'Stick an upstairs on at the back and connect through, so we can have two extra bedrooms and another bathroom above the dining room.'

'Well, I don't see a lot of point in that. Wouldn't the two bedrooms in the front be enough?'

'No.'

'But I don't quite see what good it will do you. I mean, how will you get to those new upper rooms. Will you use a ladder of some kind?'

'No, the existing stairs.'

'The levels are all different. It won't be feasible.'

'We thought of that, then Gerry – that's my son-in-law – had a brilliant idea. He suggested a sort of mezzanine for the bathrooms and steps from a gallery down into the main front bedroom.'

'I don't understand.'

The whole concept is explained to him several times and illustrated with some of Gerry's rough sketches. Eventually, the penny drops.

'Split level!' he cries, in triumph.

'You've got it!'

'Can't do it. Too dangerous.'

'Why?'

'The gallery bit. There'll be a three-foot drop. Somebody could fall over the edge.'

'We'll put a banister rail along it to prevent that.'

'Oh, I see. Rather clever, that.'

And he's the one who wins Civic Trust award for his sympathetic design.

Builders

Builders are a race apart. In some respects, their skill is staggering. They can lay bricks, for example, at such a rapid rate, and with such precision, that a whole house can spring up in a matter of hours. Let one loose with a JCB, on the other hand, and he will play in it for weeks, doing nothing more than digging a little trench for the drains. In the process he will demolish a shed, block half the street with his heap of soil and run over his own car. Building firms come in all shapes and sizes, from Perce, the local one-man firm, to the giant multinationals which reshape our city skylines.

The most infuriating thing about builders, and they are all equally guilty, is their timing. The only thing they ever do promptly is post their invoices. With everything else, whatever notice you give and however carefully you try to pin them down to a completing date, they will always be weeks late.

Conversing with builders and understanding the nuances of their conversation is a fine art. You should learn as much as you can about this. Your survival may depend on it. Here are some of the more common phrases.

Builder 'We shall start work on Wednesday morning at eight o'clock. The whole job will be done by the end of the month.'

Meaning Some time on Wednesday morning we will park our lorry on the softest part of the lawn and spread scaffolding poles all over the garden, with special heaps in front of doors and on paths. Our three men, having unloaded, will take an hour's break, scatter fruit pie packets around and then drive off in the lorry, leaving a second set of ruts in the lawn. You won't see hide nor hair of them again until three months have passed and an application for an interim payment has been made.

Builder 'We may have to cut your water supply off, love. Just for half an hour.'

Meaning Sid's just pulled the JCB bucket through the water main, we can't find the stopcock, let alone the other end of the fractured pipe, and we'll be floundering around for a day or so until the water authority can come to find the pipe route with their special detector.

Builder 'It's not the job what costs, lady, it's renting the scaffolding.'

Builder 'No need for a written estimate, my duck. It's only a little job.'

Builder 'I've done thousands of these in my time. It's little more than a five-minute job.'

Builder 'Shouldn't be too expensive, as long as we can find a reasonable brickie/chippy/glazier/plasterer/stonemason.'

All meaning This is going to cost you a king's ransom and take for ever.

Builder 'Hubby away a lot, is 'e, ducks?'

Meaning 'Services other than erecting scaffolding are available if required.'

Builder 'You on the phone, luv?'

Meaning We want to use your house as a company office for a few weeks, making sixteen phone calls a day and tramping mud all over your carpet.

Builder 'There we are, madam. Job done.'

Meaning There is a wasteland of tortured subsoil, reminiscent of the Somme. In the middle of it, concealed by piles of broken bricks, abandoned pipework, empty cement bags and bent scaffolding poles, is the completed building/extension/outbuilding or whatever.

Builder 'Of course, we'll clean up.'

Meaning We'll remove anything of value from the site but leave everything else exactly as described in the last translation.

Builders never begin an outdoor project until midwinter and never mix cement unless frost is forecast. They are fuelled by a mixture of fruit pies and Radio One and can work effectively only if the top portions of their buttocks are constantly exposed – nothing obscene, just the top part of the cleft. They dance about with gay abandon on catwalks and planks at dizzy heights without the slightest concern but will run screaming with terror from a building inhabited by a single wasp. They will fight to the death over whether someone has borrowed a wheelbarrow without permission but are happy to lend anyone a £90,000 crane for as long as he likes – as long as a few pound notes change hands. Above all, builders adore special terminology.

Using the right terms in building is rather like using the right words for different bits of a car when you are associating with autobores or naming ropes properly when among yachtsmen. It may be just a front door to you, but to a builder it's a natural-look teak half-glazed Kentucky. When talking to builders, you need to know that Anna Glypta is not an actress and that PAR has nothing whatever to do with a golf handicap. A few essential terms are explained below.

Acoustic plaster Plaster designed to amplify the sound of next door's stereo, bedsprings, etc.

Architrave The function of searching for the right architect (cf. Treasuretrave).

Arris Literally sharp or pointed. Named after the builder Erbert Arris, whose pointed remarks became legendary in the nineteenth century.

Ashlar Finely dressed stone – as opposed to rag stone which isn't and rubble walls where the stone is always used in the raw.

Baffle To confuse.

Bit 1. An attractive female. 2. Part of something – usually illegal: bit of spare; bit on the side.

Chimney gutter Someone who guts chimneys.

Coursing joint A club for field sportsmen.

Diatomaceous earth The right soil type for growing weightwatchers' vegetables.

Door furniture Pieces of furniture made from old doors.

Double glazing Domestic mould incubators.

Feather tongue Early-morning symptom caused by excessive alcohol intake the night before.

Flemish bond An example of off-shore investment where the fund is tied up in foreign bricks.

Flying scaffold Scaffolding which has become detached from the building and is somewhere between where it is supposed to be and the ground.

Italian tiling A method of tiling where the grouting is done with fresh pasta.

Lath Thcottish for a young girl.

Louvre A famous art gallery and museum in Paris.

Lump hammer A large, heavy hammer used to flatten builders' imperfections. Popular among cowboy outfits – hence the term 'lump' builders.

Mason's joint A club for policemen.

Norman Brick A well-known TV personality.

O ring A form of poetic language – 'O ring out wild bells', etc.

Rendering Giving over – 'Render unto Caesar', etc.

Spokeshave World famous sixteenth-century carpenter poet who, besides creating such immortal masterpieces as *Measure 4 Measure, The Merchant of Veneer* and *Timeshare of Athens*, invented a plane for smoothing thin bits of wood.

Staffordshire blues A jazz tune made famous by the late Holly Billiday.

Stay bar A pub with bedrooms.

Termite Mineral used in making welding rods.

Thatcher A man (or woman) of straw.

Thatcher's labourer An ex-member of the cabinet.

Veneer Fifteenth-century Flemish painter.

Welsh groin An occupational ailment suffered mainly by rugby forwards.

By now you should have enough knowledge to be able to deal with the professionals. Just to check on your progress, try these exercises.

1 How do you tell the difference between a solicitor and barrister?

2 If you wanted to start a building firm, what would be your first move?

3 In this group, who is odd man out? William of Sens, Wren, Vanbrugh, Le Corbusier.

Answers

1 Barristers serve real champagne at their drinks parties.

2 Buy a pair of trousers with no waist.

3 Le Corbusier – which is a brand of Cognac. All the rest were architects.

Chapter 3

What Services Are There?

Service is not included.

(Once stamped on every bill at Fortnum & Mason's
restaurant)

'Hullo. Is that the Eastern Water Authority?'
  'Yes.'
  'I wish to report a flood.'
  'Ah. You'll need our Corby office. This is Stamford.'
  'Oh. Well, it's rather urgent. Water is running down the street
and it's beginning to come under my back door. Can you give me
the number?'
  'Certainly, it's Corby 712372.'

'Hullo. Is that the EWA?'
  'Yes.'
  'I want to report a flood.'
  'Ah. You've dialled the wrong number.'
  'Really? This is the number Stamford gave me.'
  'You must be mistaken, sir. We don't have a Mr Stamford on
our staff.'
  'I've got a flood. Water's pouring into my kitchen from the road
outside –'
  'Off the road?'
  'Into the kitchen and rising by the minute. My carpets are
getting ruined. It's over my feet.'

'Be reasonable, sir. It is raining. There's bound to be a bit of surface water about.'

'Please help me. Something's got to be done. Fast.'

'Off the road, you say?'

'Can you do something?'

'Well, strictly speaking, "off the road" means it's a highway problem. I should contact the highway authority.'

'I thought you were responsible for water.'

'Not off the highway, that's what we call "run off". By the way, you must not make use of any of that water. Without an abstraction licence, that would be an offence. We'd have to prosecute.'

'Hullo. Highway Authority?'

'Yes.'

'There's a flood. I –'

'Sorry. You've dialled the highway office. You need the water authority.'

'They've just told me to ring you. Water's pouring off the street into my kitchen. It's up to my ankles and rising fast.'

'Ah. You need our works depot. It's in Nettlerash. Hold on, I'll find the number . . . Here we are. Nettlerash 261. Ask for Bert.'

'Hullo. Is that the Nettlerash depot?'

'Could be.'

'Is Bert there, please?'

'Ooh wants 'im?'

'I've got water flooding in.'

'Water? Piss off, mate. This is roads.'

'Hullo. Nettlerash 261? You hung up on me. Look, I am standing in my kitchen – installed last month by Smallpiece and worth a few K, I might add – water is pouring off your road and is now up to my knees. Outside, I can see my garden furniture floating away towards the Old Rectory. I'm cold. I'm wet. I'm worried. I'M GETTING PRETTY ANGRY! WILL YOU DO SOMETHING NOW?'

'All right. All right. Keep yer bloomin 'air on. Look, the whole

crew's out mending a 'ole. You wouldn't want to waste their time
in your kitchen when there's a 'ole in the B1151, now would –'

'Hold on. There's someone at the door. It'll take me a minute
to wade over. Don't hang up. *Please* don't hang up.'

At the door:

'Hullo, 'ullo, 'ullo. What's all this, then? Don't you know
there's a serious flood on?'

'Oh, thank God you've come, Constable. The water is rising
but I can't get anyone to come to see to it.'

'There's a blocked drain out there, sir. It's pouring off the hill
and coming straight down the main street. Cor. You must have
a foot or more in this room. Why haven't you got the authorities
here?'

'What authorities?'

'Water, fire brigade, highways.'

'Aaah! I've been trying all morning. No one wants to know.
I'm going bananas here!'

'Not been living here very long, have you, sir? Not used to
country ways?'

'Dear God! How can I ma –'

'May I use the phone, sir? Oh, I see you are on it now.'

'Oh, that's the Nettlerash depot. There's no one there. They're
all out mending a hole, except for a complete cretin. I expect he's
too stupid even to fill in holes.'

'Just give me the phone, sir. Hullo, that you, Martin? Call up
the crew on yer radio and send 'em to Nether Sodding. Tell 'em
to get a wiggle on, there's a bad flood 'ere. Oh, and while you're
on, tell yer Mum I'll be home at two. Bye.'

'Thank you, Constable.'

'You could 'ave done that yerself, sir. Do yerself a favour. Next
time there's a flood, ring the Water Board first, before it gets this
far.'

'Well, really!'

'And another thing. That – what did you call 'im? – "total
cretin" is my son. He's got three 'A' levels. In fact 'e's only filling
in time at the depot before he goes up to Jesus –'

'Oh. Taking Holy Orders, is he?'

'Jesus College, Cambridge, sir.'

'Not been living here very long, have you sir? Not
used to country ways. . . ?'

Writing a whole chapter about rural services is going to be difficult because there aren't any. The real art of country survival is not so much developing your self-sufficiency as identifying those people upon whom you will come to depend.

Services to your home can never be taken for granted. Most houses have eccentricities and usually, the older the house, the odder the services. My own house was built in the days when nobody washed from October to May. They covered themselves with goose grease and sewed themselves into their underwear. In fact, it is common knowledge among eminent social historians that the clothes peg was used for hanging out washing only as a secondary function. The name has changed through a corruption in the language and the original 'close pegge' was used to restrict the nostrils during social intercourse. (The other kind was out of the question, since folk were stitched into their underwear.) What all this boils down to is that any house built before the Napoleonic Wars is not designed to accommodate modern ideas of comfort and personal hygiene.

Water

All old country houses have an unwavering attraction for water. They encourage it in through leaky roofs, under window ledges and through cracks in the masonry. Pipes drip, undetected in concealed cavities, for years until suddenly, on the day you expect twenty to dinner, fifteen gallons of filthy, stagnant water crashes through the ceiling on to your table centre just as you are arranging the last pink button rose. Most old buildings indulge in a 'what I have, I hold' philosophy. They cling to waste water and sewage with as much tenacity as the Americans at El Alamo. Few are on mains drainage – because mains drainage is uncommon in the countryside – and most systems developed since the days of the privy are simply not up to handling modern needs. The traditional closed cesspool, for example, depended on a family of six having five baths a year and not going to the loo more than once a week each. Nowadays, with people worrying about BO, not to mention all the high fibre bread and muesli everyone's into, the average cesspool needs emptying once a week.

The alternative is a septic tank, but be warned! Get the levels wrong and you are in deep sh . . . er, trouble. Our house is built into a hillside so that the lower kitchen is below ground level on one side. Since, when we arrived, our waste flowed into a disused well, it seemed appropriate to modernise the system. Fearing the ineptitude of cowboy builders, we went to the top, employing a highly reputable local firm who, being experts with old properties, were frequently employed to repair and restore ancient churches and cathedrals. A little job like installing our drains, they told us breezily, would be completed without fuss in a few days. 'Go on holiday while we do it,' suggested the enthusiastic young director. 'Then, when you come back, it will be all complete.' We fixed the starting date and went to Cornwall!

When we got back, tired from a week of steady rain and that particular brand of surly inhospitality reserved by the Cornish for use on their visitors, the garden looked like an open-face coal mine.

'We've had the most dreadful problems,' said the director, his enthusiasm a trifle more forced than before. 'We met bare rock.'

'I'm not surprised,' I said. 'This is a limestone area. I thought you knew.'

'We've had to drill with jack-hammers. For days!'

'Not all finished, then?'

'Not quite.'

'How long?'

'Hard to say. A week. Ten days. A month perhaps.'

'Oh, well.' I sensed he needed some conciliatory noises from me. 'At least the old system is still connected. We can survive with that for a while longer while you sort yourself out.'

'Ah, well, er, there's a slight problem there. We've cut all that off.'

'So we have no drains at all?'

'Well, no.'

'Whose idea was it to do things that way round?'

'The site manager's. He thought, as you were on holiday, it wouldn't matter. He cut the old drain when the building inspector came to tell us to replace the new underground pipework.'

'Replace the *new* pipework?'

'The plastic pipe we were supplied with just wasn't strong enough. It collapsed under the weight of the soil.'

'Was that the pipe my wife had to sign for?'

'That's right. She said it looked a bit flimsy.'

'Yes, she did. I also remember her being annoyed when your site manager advised her not to worry her pretty head and to leave such things to the menfolk.'

'Yes, er, there is also the problem of the, ah, levels.'

'The "A" levels?'

'It seems we've dug the hole for the tank a bit deep. Water won't flow along the outfall.'

'But if that level is wrong, the whole system is caput.'

'I'm afraid so. I'm very sorry.'

'What are we going to do?'

'Well, there is one possibility.'

'Really?'

'Yes, sir. A pump.'

'A pump?'

'That's right. All we need do is pump the foul water up and away. Of course, there'll be maintenance problems and running costs, but it's the best we can do in the circumstances.'

'What do I and my family do while you sort out this mess?'

'Er, I don't suppose you'd care to take a few more days holiday, would you, sir?'

In ten years we've had four different types of pump and once nearly lost an electrician's apprentice when he was 'volunteered' to climb down into the sump to inspect the suction pipe. When they got him out, what he was covered with was not glory.

Plumbers

As soon as you have moved in, you must start to investigate even the vaguest rumours of a local plumber. If you are lucky enough to have one within driving distance, invite him over for a drink, make sure he is on the guest list of your first dinner party and never, never fail to send him a bottle of whisky at Christmas. You must ensure that he is permanently in your debt, even if that means paying his bills before he ever actually does anything. You must do this because you are bound to need his services at the most unlikely times. Pipes burst only at night, heating systems go wrong the day before Christmas Eve and drains block on Good Friday. When he dashes in to save you from yet another flood, don't be surprised if he arrives in white tie and tails. Because of his professional standing, he will be moving in more exalted social circles than you are able to aspire to and will be going on from your pipes to the Lord Mayor's banquet. Incidentally, if your own career begins to pall, plumbing could be an attractive alternative for you, once you've passed your City and Guilds – no, not in plumbing, silly; in accountancy. If you take up plumbing, you'll soon have some large capital funds to manage!

If all this dependence on water pipes and plumbers tempts you to go native and live on spring water, just bear two points in mind. First, bottled spring water has been irradiated to kill off the bugs. Second, drink pure water from the well in the garden and you are courting disaster. Sheep and cattle constantly defecate and urinate on the ground from which your well is fed. No problem there – it's all good organic matter – but they also shed liver flukes and once these are in your body, you've got them for keeps. Wild watercress is deadly. The larval stages of the liver fluke sit on the leaves waiting for a customer, so however tempting the green crop at the edge of the brook may be, you must not eat it unless you want to get fluked. Look up the biology of *Fasciola hepatica* and you will never eat watercress again – unless you want your internal organs to play host to parasites the size of 35 mm colour slides!

Electricity: Energy for Life

Doesn't it drive you doolally-tap to see those *infuriating* advertisements for electricity? What are they trying to prove? Why do they spend millions telling us how wonderful electricity is when, for most everyday activities, we have no alternative but to use it. How many homes have hurricane lamps in their drawing rooms these days? Who ever heard of a water-powered vacuum cleaner?

Or do they think there are still people out there who have not
yet discovered the joys of this modern energy source. Can't you
picture them, these poor souls, hand-weaving garments in candlelight and behaving as though they were acting in brown bread
commercials. But even then the electricity adverts would be a
stupid waste of money, because such people would never see
them.

When you move in, the chances are you'll want to rewire your
house. The electrician inspecting your obsolete ring main will tell
you that every appliance is a potential deathtrap; that anyone
taking a shower would be lucky to come out alive; and that
rodents have eaten through the insulation on the main cable. He'll
mystify you with technical jargon, scattering his conversation with
confusing terms like 'PME', 'polarity' and 'single phase'. 'The
firm what put this lot in went bust five years ago,' he might say.
''ardly surprising when you think o' that noo supermarket they
burnt down.' Naturally, you'll decide to play safe and go for a
completely new system.

Once the house has been rewired, the electrician will tell you
it's safer than ever. No one could get a shock off the lights because
the super-sensitive earth would trip before the current got half-
way out of the socket, never mind up your arm. An instinct of
self-preservation tells you to take him at his word and not to put
your fingers in the light socket anyway. However, just as you are
sinking gratefully into a large whisky and soda, having seen the
electrical workers off the premises, the lights all go out. It's the
sensitive trip. It goes off a couple more times that evening and
again in the night, nobbling your alarm clock-radio and letting
the deepfreeze contents melt. The electrician returns next day
with a gadget which he sticks into all the plug holes. He reports
his findings.

'Everything seems to be in good order, sir. Are you *sure* the
lights kept going off?'

'Not completely sure, no. I might have been hallucinating or
struck with intermittent blindness.'

'Ah.'

'Did you find a fault?'

'Well, not an actual fault you could lay your hands on, no, sir.'

'So it could happen again?'

'Oh no, sir. If there'd been anything wrong, we'd 'ave picked it up with this gismo.'

They depart. All is well until evening. Just when you have finished putting new stocks of food into the deepfreeze, the lights all go off. This time, the trip won't go back on. You ring the electrician, who, two hours later – about nine pm to be precise – returns in a surly mood.

'Yer trip's gorn,' he says, opening the fuse board cover. 'Just wants putting back on.'

Though it wouldn't go on for you, he presses the button and on come all the lights. You apologise, he goes and fifteen minutes later the lights go out. You haven't the nerve to ring him again and spend the rest of the evening in candlelight. Next day, you ring again. He comes promptly but is decidedly fed up by this time.

'You haven't any weird things on, have you?'

'What, under this sweater and these jeans, you mean?'

'No, mate. I mean have you got an arc welder or anything like that?'

'Oh, absolutely. I spend my life welding arks. In fact, my middle name is Noah!'

'I meant anything with a faulty connection. How is your toaster, for example?'

'Redundant.'

'Eh?'

'Useless!'

'Ah, well, say ner mo-er! It's yer faulty toaster.'

'You misunderstand. It's redundant because I have no electricity.'

Your sarcasm is lost on him. He explains that what you must do now is to turn everything off and then work through the house turning things back on until the trip goes. You try it but nothing goes wrong. You try again. Still nothing goes wrong. He leaves you and within an hour the switch has tripped. Eventually they put the old, insensitive trip switch back and everything works perfectly from that point on. The trouble is, you spend a lot of time thinking that whatever made the other one trip might be a potential fire hazard. One night you wake in a cold sweat, thinking you can hear flames crackling, but it turns out to be nothing more

than the noise of water from a burst pipe trickling down the back
stairs.

Gas: Energy for Suicide

If the electricity advertisements are infuriating, what about gas?
Advertising something we all use is maddening enough, but in the
country you can't *get* gas. Thus the gas board spends millions of
pounds exhorting you to use a product which they are not prepared to let you have. Although nobody can use gas in the
countryside, vast areas have been given over to huge pipes carrying it from one city to another. If you farm land with a gas pipeline
running through your fields, it is a good idea to wear a crash
helmet and parachute in case the worst happens – the crash helmet
to protect your head when you are blown through the tractor cab
roof and the parachute for a safe landing.

Heating the House

Besides an addiction to water, old houses hate warmth. They shed
heat with enthusiasm and, though you may have spent thousands
on insulation and draughtproofing, you will still be quite unable
to feel warm between the months of November and April. Stone
houses are cold in winter and hot in summer, brick buildings are
draughty and thatched roofs, though good at insulation, inhibit
you from lighting fires because you are too terrified of being burnt
alive. So you might as well face facts: either you will be spending
a great deal of money every winter heating passing aeroplanes or
you will need to be guardian of the definitive overcoat and woolly
collection.

There are no cheap solutions. Gentry who do not live in London
eke out a miserable existence in the smallest of their reception
rooms, crouched over massive log fires which do little more than

keep condensation off the walls. Guests are issued with trench coats so that, in the unfortunate event of a trip to the lavatory being necessary, they will not suffer from exposure on the way. You'll notice, when hobnobbing with noble families, that they never take ice in their drinks and would rather die than be seen tucking into ice cream. This is not, as you might suppose, on grounds of decorum but because they have a natural horror of cold. Who wouldn't, living in those conditions? After all, the Eskimo's hell is a cold place.

Choosing the right form of heating in your country house is important because different systems suit different houses. Of all fuels, gas is best. But you can't get gas in the country, so whatever else you choose will be less than satisfactory.

Electricity is expensive. Night storage heaters are fine for warming the rodents during their nocturnal antics but by the time you return, tired and shirty after your long journey from work, the heaters will be cold. Modern versions have a boost gadget which is supposed to store the heat until you need it, but you always forget to adjust it last thing at night, so the heat dissipates during the day.

If you have invested in a large house, electricity will cost even more. Unlike other businesses which offer discounts to big purchasers, gas and electricity penalise their better customers by making them pay more per unit. So unless you are very rich or have bought a very small, well-insulated cottage, electric heating is not advisable.

Wood fires are romantic. They are also inefficient, dirty, smelly and expensive to run. Every chimney built before 1880 smokes. The inglenook fireplace is an ingenious invention which enables the heat of the fire to be separated from the smoke. The former goes up the chimney; the latter fills the room. In the days when people were stitched into their goose-greasy underwear, a fire that belched a constant supply of acrid woodsmoke provided a welcome diversion from the other odours. Nowadays we dislike streaming eyes and black faces, so if you intend to use wood fires, you will need to reconstruct your fireplaces and chimneys.

Lighting your first fire is an adventure. All may be going well downstairs, but nip up to your bedroom to fetch a book and you could be horrified to find a thick fog up there. Go outside and

the sight of smoke coming out *through* the roof slates is even
more unnerving. If this happens, you have a chimney-lining problem. The lining of your pocket will be hit too, but since the smoke
has got into your wardrobe and made all your smart clothes smell
like ashtray-flavoured kippers, you know something will have to
be done.

Nowadays, chimney lining is a relatively simple matter but, my
dear, the cost! The procedure is fascinating to watch, if slightly
pornographic in its connotations. They thread a long rubber tube
down the inside of the flue from top to bottom. A couple of holes
have to be bashed in the wall so that the experts can see into the
void. Then they fill the whole cavity with sloshy goo, which sets
like cement. Before it sets, and this is the intriguing bit, they
inflate the tube with compressed air. The effect is to force the
goo into all the cracks and chinks between the stones or bricks
and to create a perfect flue at the same time. Watching them
deflate and remove the tube is quite disgusting – especially if
you've got a dirty mind – but after a couple of days you are
allowed to light a fire and spot the difference. No more fog in the
bedroom; no more kippered dresses. And no more fires – because
the chimney doesn't draw at all now that the diameter of its flue
has been changed!

Assuming you have a wood fire that does work, where are you
going to go for your logs? Just pop off to the nearest copse with
a chainsaw? Not exactly. All wood, including the rotted bits lying
about on the ground, belongs to somebody. Even if you are on
the remotest stretch of the moors, not a dwelling in sight for miles
around, and just happen to pick up a few old twigs and little
branches, some tortured soul will leap out from behind a gorse
bush and shout, 'Oi! Whaddya thinkya doing wi' that wood?'

'Collecting it. It's lying about.'

'So it is.'

'Well, mayn't I just pick up these few bits?'

'No.'

'Why not?'

'S'mine.'

Buying firewood is even more expensive than buying coal. 'Best
Logs' – the local paper might say – '£45 per load delivered.' You
ring the number to be told that a 'load' means a trailerful brought

by tractor. You order. Eventually a tractor arrives pulling an empty trailer. When you look into the trailer you discover that it is not completely empty. There's a layer of logs in the bottom.

'Is that a full load?' you ask incredulously.

'Yes, ma'am,' says the driver, a roll-your-own-fag in the corner of his mouth.

'I thought there might be more.'

'There's a ton 'n' alf here. S'a big trailer. Wherejawannem?'

'In that shed, please. Would you like some coffee?'

'Oh ah!' You go indoors to make coffee. While you pour water from the kettle you hear a rumble outside. The trailer is upended and the logs, which you now realize form a formidable heap, are on the ground right outside the front door.

'What have you done?' you ask, your consternation sharpened because you have lunch guests arriving within half an hour.

'Shootin' yer load.'

'But you asked where I wanted them.'

'Ah. So's I'd know where to shoot 'em.'

'Aren't you going to put them in the shed?'

'Noo, lady. Tha's stackin. I only shoot 'em. I don't reckon ter stack.'

'How am I supposed to get them in there?'

'Aincher gotta wheelbarrer?'

There are ancient sayings about which wood is best and which to avoid for open fires, but in practice all wood is scarce and precious so it pays to be content with anything as long as it will burn. Willow spits a lot and elm burns slowly and sulkily but they all put out heat. By the way, don't be tempted to invest in a wood-burning stove. They pollute the atmosphere with uncombusted carcinogens and clog up chimney flues with material which looks like oxtail soup and smells worse than a Fisherman's Friend, especially when it starts to ooze through the wallpaper. Not only that; they're hideously ugly and most un-British!

'I only shoot 'em. I don't reckon ter stack.'

Oil-fired Central Heating

Because gas is absent from rural areas and electricity so expensive, country houses which have any central heating at all will usually be oil fired. There are several things wrong with oil:

1 It has to be stored in a large tank in the garden.

2 This always goes rusty and eventually springs a leak, killing everything in the garden and poisoning the wildlife.

3 It smells disgusting.

4 Oil boilers go funny in freezing weather, failing when you need them most.

5 Oil boilers are expensive to maintain and the maintenance contractors are usually recalcitrant and elusive.

6 Oil deliveries are difficult to time – either you run out before the tanker arrives or you have too much left and have to pay a premium because they can't fit your order into your tank.

Siting the oil tank is problematic because if you try to conceal it in an out-of-the-way corner, it will be inaccessible for the tanker. If you site it for easy delivery, it will probably blot the light out of your sitting room. If you try to compromise, placing it in a convenient spot but growing clematis over it, the oil man will mangle the clematis just when its blooms are looking their best and the plant itself will hasten the spread of rust, and hence its own end when the tank begins to leak. The longer the pipeline to the house, the more likely the oil is to congeal in winter, ruining the boiler but, if the tank is too near, smells will filter indoors, blending with those from the septic tank. Besides, if there's a house fire, how will you feel about the proximity of 3,000 gallons of fuel oil?

If you move into a house which is already heated by an oil-fired system, you will need a maintenance contract. When the engineer arrives, you can expect him to be unimpressed:

'This it then?'

'Yes indeed.'

'Oh dear oh dear oh dear!'

'Anything wrong?'

'Everything. They gave up making this model in 1980. Never did get it right.'

'Oh.'

'Last people had a lot of trouble with this. Design's all wrong, you see.'

'Really?'

'Yeah. Chimney flue's the wrong shape for the baffles and the jets on this model are virtually impossible to adjust. Then there's yer stat. Never have managed to put in a good stat, this firm.'

'Well, you'll have to do what you can, anyway.'

'Not only that, she's well under capacity. You'd need half a million for this place, I'll be bound.'

'Oh well, we've only just moved in. It's not for sale really I mea –'

'Bri'ish Thermal Units – you need half a million BTUs. How many rads 'yer got?'

'Heavens, I've no idea.'

'Well, I expect this machine to give us nothing but trouble.'

'Perhaps we ought to think about a new boiler.'

'Good thought, sir! This one's on its last legs anyway.'

Weeks later, after doing your research, you will have a brand new boiler. In triumph, you ring your oil company to arrange for the maintenance engineer to come out and inspect your purchase.

'Thermolux 600!' he says.

'Yes, rather grand, don't you think?'

'Oh dear oh dear oh dear!'

'It's fully automatic. There's even a computer to work out how much hot water is needed before you know yourself.'

'Oh dear oh dear oh dear.'

'You don't seem impressed.'

'These are nothing but trouble. They haven't got the bugs out of the design yet. So new, you see.'

'Oh Lor!'

'But what I can't understand, sir, is why you got rid of your old boiler. Good machine, that was. Years o' life in it yet.'

Having had a brief glance at some of the internal services in country houses, you will need to satisfy yourself that reasonable bus and train services exist. Also, how far away does your local policeman live? What are the local roads like? Is the house on a milk round? What about bread? Papers? Jehovah's Witnesses?

Country bus services used to be something of a joke. That was before privatization. Now they do not exist. If you are lucky enough to live on a school route, there may be two buses a day, designed to coincide with the beginning and end of the school day. Country buses are always late. Well, nearly always. The one time you don't get to the bus stop on time, the bus will have passed through ten minutes early. The maddening thing is that because so few people use the bus, you won't know it's gone and will stand there for an hour thinking it's late as usual.

Although there are very few left, you may be lucky enough to live near a railway. A quarter of a century ago, the concept of the railway as a service for passengers was abandoned. Today each county has one rural station and one in the city. Kemble, for example, serves the whole of rural Gloucestershire. The alternative is a long drive to Cheltenham, where the parking of vehicles anywhere is expressly forbidden, or jagging down the M5 to Bristol. There, the station is at a place called Brishmeads. This is a corruption of the Old English Bristol Temple Meads and conjures up the idea of pastoral scenes with naked shepherds dancing with nymphs in a bosky landscape. In fact, Brishmeads is a storm-battered platform with a prefab on one side where everyone huddles out of the weather, waiting for their train. The only place on earth colder than Brishmeads is Peterborough Station.

Rumours of rural train services coming back are completely unfounded and have been put about by estate agents who are trying to push up country house prices. However, British Rail have introduced cross-country trains called sprinters. These are modern, two-carriage affairs, so called because they travel at the speed of a sprinting man. They have space-age loos festooned with ambiguous instructions, buttons and flashing lights designed to frighten off all but the most desperate. They also have charming hostesses, who wheel trolleys up and down proffering sweets, bikkies, an occasional sandwich and the most disgusting instant coffee imaginable. The trolleys have been designed for maximum awkwardness, needing the strength of Samson to wheel and having sharp corners at passenger elbow level. A trip from Birmingham to Harwich in a sprinter train could lead to your losing a whole arm if you sit in an aisle seat.

Policing the countryside is difficult when there is only one Bobby per county. Phone for help and your local officer could be miles away, interviewing someone about a shotgun licence – speaking of which, you may need to apply for a firearms certificate yourself. To do this you'll need to apply to the police, who will interview you in your home. The interview will go something like this.

'Hullo, 'ullo, 'ullo.'

'Ah, good afterble, Constanoon! I locked myself out and was just trying to get in through my own window.'

'I believe you, sir. Mr Coletorn, is it? Mr Neil Coletorn?'

'Up to a point.'

'You applied for a firearms certificate?'

'Oh yes. Do come in. Oh, you can't, I'm locked out.'

'No matter, sir. Bit of a dab hand at getting in, I am. May I?'

'Please do. Good Lord. How on earth did you do that?'

'Trick of the trade, sir. Wouldn't be fair to show you.'

'But I've just had new security locks fitted.'

'So I see, sir. Very prudent. After you, sir.'

'Thank you, Constable. Oh, I beg your pardon, Sergeant. Do come in. Sit down.'

'Thank you, sir. Now.' Out of his pocket comes form and notebook. 'Just a few questions.'

'Fire away. Oh, ha ha. My little joke, you understand!'

'I see, sir. Now then, er, are you given to fits of violent temper?'

'Oh, absolutely. All the time, usually with the children.'

'I see, sir. Have you any pet hates?'

'Lord, yes. Hundreds.'

'Could you name a few?'

'Certainly. Fuchsias, bad architecture, racial intolerance, sherry trifle, Mickey Rooney films – that do for a few samples?'

'I meant people really.'

'Oh, I see. Um, people who smoke in trains, the Prime Minister – well, everyone in the cabinet really – the Leader of the Opposition, the Mayor, all bishops – well, perhaps not –'

'Thank you, sir. I think I get the picture. Is this just in your mind or would you actually do anything rash?'

'Oh, you bet your life I would. I always draw specs and moustaches on their photos.'

'Where would you keep the weapon?'

'Oh, lying about, I expect. I mean I'd try to remember to lock it up but I'm so terribly forgetful.'

'Are people likely to wander on to the area you've designated as being the spot where you'll be discharging your weapon?'

'You mean where I want to shoot? Oh, I expect so. They're always trespassing down there, picking blackberries, mushrooms, canoodling and so on. Bloody riff-raff!'

'Quite, sir. Do you know what the killing range of your rifle would be?'

'Oh, I'm such a rotten shot, officer, I think the bunny rabbits will be quite safe with me, what? Ha ha!'

'It can kill at up to a mile, sir.'

'Really? Good Lord, I'd no idea!'

'Well, that's all I need to ask at this stage, sir. Of course, your application will have to be approved by my superiors but, informally, I can tell you that you'll have no problems. You seem just the sort of person who should be allowed to have a rifle.'

'Oh, you're too kind, con-sergeant.'

'We do have to be careful and I'm sorry I had to ask such difficult questions. We want to keep weapons out of the hands of the wrong people, don't we, sir? I mean, your criminal classes and irresponsible types.'

'Oh, abso*lut*ely, sergeant.'

By now you should realise that services in the country are as plentiful as English test match victories. If you want good services, don't live in the country. Live in Kensington.

Just to make sure you have got the message, here are a few little exercises.

1 Dial 999, ask for the police and then set your stop watch. If they arrive within half an hour you are in a pretty well-served area. Do tell the officers who arrive why you called them. They will be grateful to know how well they did.

2 Set fire to your garden shed and then try the same with the fire

brigade. (You don't have to ignite the shed really, but it's best to have an actual fire somewhere on the premises to avoid a row.)

3 You are seventy-nine years old and do not drive. A bus runs from your village to Norwich, twenty miles away, every Wednesday afternoon. You need to visit your relative in Llandinam, central Wales. You cannot afford a taxi. How will you do it? (Limit your answer to three sides of A4 paper if you can.)

Chapter 4

Fitting In

Well, perhaps I shall like it in Casablanca.

(Paul Henreid as Victor Laszlo in the film *Casablanca*,
Warner Bros, 1942)

You won't fit in, you know. Not at first. Whatever your background, you'll be regarded as a foreigner. Some areas are worse than others. In East Anglia, natives treat outsiders with a sort of pitying contempt. In the north of England, where apart from York and Harrogate, which are posh, everywhere is a bit down-market, people are plain-spoken – well, rude really – but at the same time helpful and welcoming. Cotswold people are superior to everybody else and now that Royals have taken to living there, they speak only to them or to God.

Within this regional variation, individual villages are strongly contrasting. One community can be warm and loving, embracing new inhabitants with enthusiasm, when a mile away, you could move in and be spoken to by nobody for the first thirty years of your residence. Of course, your own attitude will be very important and this chapter is intended to show how you can become a supportive and worthwhile member of your village.

The secret lies in getting to know the rural psyche. The archetypal native is the **Born Countryman**. A BC is likely to be a farmer or at least to have agricultural connections, but whatever he is, he earns his living in the country. A BC knows that, unlike town people, he has common sense and is down to earth. He can watch animals coupling in the fields without fainting. He knows exactly what needs doing to thieves, bank robbers, insider dealers, homosexuals and politicians. He claims to have an innate understanding of the rhythm of the countryside – which is odd, because all his favourite country pursuits involve killing animals. Since his intellect is already superior to the townee's, he has no need to improve it by reading. Things like acid rain, the 'greenhouse' effect and holes in the ozone layer are no problem to him, because he knows that they are caused by alarmist muckrakers who live on twigs and muesli instead of good, healthy things like fatty bacon, cream and lager. He also knows that people who move out into country areas are naïve enough to be conned in all sorts of ways. The art of integrating into his sort of society, if you really want to, is to keep feeding him with the idea that he has got you by the short and curlies, even if he hasn't.

The **Rural Commuter** has more in common with you. She (or he) has lived – sometimes for generations – in the country but earns her income by going to work every day in the local town. This contact with the outside world enables her to have a more open mind than the BC, who may only visit his local market town twice a year. She does a lot for the village and may well be a keen gardener or have some other absorbing rural hobby, like watching television or crochet work. If she tells you she likes crewel work, you won't know whether she means foxhunting or stitching coloured wool on to cloth.

Your biggest threat comes from the **Salt of the Earth**. Every village has an SOE, but luckily they are usually quite easy to spot. SOEs are always found during pub opening hours propping up the bar, wagging a finger on one hand and an empty pint glass in the other. The barman will introduce you: 'You've not met old Silas yet, have you? Salt o' the Earth is Silas. Do anything for you. Any little favours, any problems, just ask Silas.' Of course, he's been thoroughly primed to say this because he clicks for 5 per cent of the winnings. SOEs are experts on absolutely everything, but in spite of their bewildering pile of accumulated knowledge, they have never bothered to get a degree or anything like that. They always have an official trade – often a strange one, like mole catcher or reed cutter – but this is usually little more than a front for the odd-jobbing and shady dealing they do for

SOEs are always found during pub opening hours
propping up the bar.

any sucker who is mug enough to take them on. Once they have caught your attention and taken a couple of pints off you, they'll start to indoctrinate you.

'Mine's a pint, please, boss.'

'Goodness, finished already? Well, you were saying about the tiles.'

'Ooh, ah! Sophiewest'ns.'

'Sophie whats?'

'That's the name o' your tiles, see.'

'Really? I thought they were just clay peg tiles.'

'Nooo, they ain't clay. More a sorta cast puggle. You'll niver find replacements. 'ey don't cast 'em no more, see.'

'Oh dear. What about the hole in my roof? I had hoped to repair it with the original tiles. The architect says they are available at the builder's merchant.'

'Architecks! Woddatheyknow? There 'asn't bin a sophiewest'n cast for years. I should know. It were my great grandfather wot cast 'em.'

'But this is a disaster. What *can* I do?'

'Well, for a start, yer can see ter this empty glass. Then, I might be able to put you on to a supply of old ones wot came off of Bert 'iggin's granary.'

'Really? That would be wonderful. What luck that we met!'

'It'll cost yer, mind.'

'Oh, no problem. Besides, I'd much rather have old, weathered tiles – so much more in keeping, don't you think.'

'Ooh ah! By the way, I usually reckon to 'ave a little rum and pep chaser about this time– just to set the deal, like.'

Having got to know the inhabitants, your next step is to familiarise yourself with the village's social structure. There will be several power bases and you will need to decide how deeply to get involved. First, there's the church. The Church of England, as in urban areas, has no power or influence over social life at all. Since only about 1 per cent of the population actually bothers to go to church, and since most advice from the bishops is not only conflicting but quite irrelevant to rural life, this is hardly surprising. However, lay people who work *within* the church at village level wield immense power. The hub of this strength is found in the

Parochial Church Council. Here, the churchwardens, treasurer and other committee members get together to decide how things are going to be run. The vicar or rector must always attend PCC meetings but he has no actual say in what goes on. His presence is tolerated rather than welcomed.

Anybody involved in politics will know that a thick skin is essential if you are to survive the mudslinging and backstabbing. But what goes on in Westminster is nothing to the carnage of a contentious PCC meeting. Sensitive souls have been carried out unconscious, never to regain their sanity. Among other quaint procedures at PCC meetings, everyone tends to address each other formally, even though they have known one another for years. If you want to play your part in village politics, be prepared for the rough stuff. You have been warned!

Secular matters are decided by the Parish Meeting or Council, which in turn is policed by an unofficial inner cabal who keep most of the power to themselves. They are there to see that the 'right sort of people' come to live in the village, and to block all planning applications other than their own. In the more feudal villages, the local aristocrat or his wife will chair all meetings, including the board of govenors of the village school, the horticultural society and, of course, the Bench. In villages where society has become 'democratised', a new squire is bound to emerge. He will probably be a local businessman and his politics will be just a touch to the right of Genghis Khan. Supported by an army of toadies, who secretly despise him and say the most damning things about him behind his back, he will lay down the law on all village matters. We'll see more of him in the next chapter but at this stage you just need to know that he exists.

Few other villagers wield the power he does but there are individuals whose clout is out of proportion to what you might imagine considering their status. The village shopkeeper, for instance, besides trading in stale groceries and withered fruit, is also the community's chief purveyor of rumour and gossip. She knows what you're up to before you know yourself. Any conversation with her must be conducted with caution because of her innate ability to transpose innocent snippets of dialogue into damaging evidence. Viz.:

'Been in our village nine months now, haven't you, Mr Redbrace?'

'Oh ya, Mrs Stickybeke. We *love* it here. In fact, we're thinking of taking the kids out of Poragelump Hall and sending them to the village school. I think learning local values is *so* important, don't you?'

'I wouldn't know, Mr Redbrace. I'm no expert in such things.'

Two minutes after he's left the shop, bearing a loaf of yesterday's bread and a box of last month's Colonel Rudyard's fancy cakes, several local wives drop in to collect the day's papers and gossip.

'Those Redbraces are in trouble,' says Ma Stickybeke. 'I told you they wouldn't last.'

'How do you know, Vi?'

'Well, for a start, they can't afford the fees at that snobby prep school any more. The kids 'ave got to go to Old Sodham Primary, poor little mites.'

'Well, what's wrong with that? We all went there.'

'Then there's the car. He didn't come in that Porsche thing. Just a Fiesta. Not new.'

'P'raps it's 'is wife's.'

'But it's not new.'

'So what?'

'Don't you see. It's August!'

'Oh ah! You're right, they must be getting short.'

'Then there's the clothes. 'e had a dirty old sweater on, full of 'oles.'

'That proves it. They're going under.'

Village shop etiquette is strange and unless you know how to behave, you could make yourself most unpopular. For instance, if a Born Countryman comes in, even if you are in the middle of your purchasing, you must step back and allow him to jump the queue. Children, on the other hand, can be pushed in front of with impunity, even if they are only in to buy a Mars Bar. If you don't push in, Ma Stickybeke will ask you what you want over their heads.

Whatever the condition of the merchandise, you do not ever pass comment. Even if you buy something in good faith but find it to be mouldy or paraffin-flavoured when you get home, you must suffer in silence rather than bring the wrath of the village shopkeeper round your ears. After a while, you will begin to develop a keen sense of which food items keep well enough to be safe to buy.

Never take your dog into the village shop. Animals are not hygienic in food shops and you will be told so quite firmly. The shopkeeper's own animals – the golden retriever sleeping on the floor next to the bread shelf and the cat curled up in the box of apples – are not a health risk because she knows exactly where they've been.

If ever a stranger walks into the shop while you are there, it is essential to carry out the following procedure:

1 Stop all conversation at once.

2 Stare unabashed at the stranger and, if possible, stand between him and the shelves so that he has to reach round you.

3 Watch carefully as he brings his goods to the counter or checkout and sprint there first so that he arrives at the tail of a queue.

4 As your turn to pay for your purchase arises, be sure to quiz the shopkeeper on the country of origin of every item, probing into the climate, political system and potential as a holiday spot in each case.

5 When you have completed your purchasing, do not leave the shop but join the other shoppers in a little circle watching the stranger pay for his goods and then following him with their eyes to the door. Just before the door closes behind him, start off a roar of conversation, peppered with raucous laughter.

Breaking the Ice at Parties

One big advantage of country living is that there are plenty of parties. People often buy houses which are far too large for them simply to be able to give good parties. As in town, there are many different categories from 'White Tie and Tails' balls to Conservative. (A Labour party has never been observed in the country. Indeed, it is said that in most of the shires, you could put a blue necktie round the handle of a vacuum cleaner and the constituents would return it to Westminster with a huge increase in majority. All that sucking up, I suppose.) The sweat and vomit affairs which frequent university campuses are almost absent from the country, but they have their upper-crust equivalent, especially among the young. Dinner parties are the most frequent affairs, with cocktail bashes coming a close second. Balls must be avoided wherever possible, but complete escape from them is not likely.

Then there are the expressly rustic affairs. Country barbecues are very popular these days and you will also need to know how to behave at shooting parties, hunt suppers, garden parties and housewarmings. Obviously, you are already quite used to parties but because there are so many opportunities for solecisms out in the sticks, it might prove helpful to run through a few kinds here.

Major parties will be celebrating important events, like weddings, comings of age or cremations. You will need to have special invitations printed, but make sure you use the right wording. A gilt-edged card which reads:

SIR JEREMY AND LADY WHITEHALL–MANDRIN
Request the pleasure of the company of

_____

at the **Coming Out** *of their son*

RODNEY

might raise a few eyebrows, especially if Rodney's boyfriend features in the text as well. It would have been better to have played safe and sent a straightforward 'At Home' card.

Invitations on ready-printed cards, especially brightly coloured ones displaying pictures of balloons and the word 'PARTY', are unthinkable except for persons under eight, but it is quite acceptable to print or write a funny one as long as it's not too corny.

Fred and Mabel Sterncleet invite you to help them lay up the yacht on Saturday 13 November at 8.30 at the *Ample Bosham* sailing club. Ship's rations provided but bring your own grog.

is almost tolerable, but

Bruce and Hilda Grassbox are thrilled to be celebrating their twelfth joyful year at *Bladderthwaite* post office and hope, so much, that you'll honour them with your presence at 8.30 on the 13th.

is a bit drecky. Some people go cryptic.

> **Get fibre fix plus ferment next Sat (13) ½ eight.**
> **Liz & Mike Hempen**

Most dinner invitations are verbal these days. This is easier in some respects, but when accosted on the phone, it's far more difficult to dodge an unwelcome fixture with someone you dislike.

'Ransidd Tallow 413.'

'Sylvia? Daphne!'

'Daphne!' (Thinks: Oh my Gawd, I know what's coming.) 'How are you? It's been such ages.'

'Hasn't it just? Look, are you doing anything on Saturday fortnight? The 13th.'

'I'm not sure.' You turn up a blank page in your diary. Now, how are you going to handle the reply? Lie through your teeth? Dissemble? 'I'm afraid we're tied up.' (Liar!) 'There's nothing in my diary but I'm sure Neville said something about a weekend conference.' (Dissembler!) Of course, you could try, 'I'm going into a spiritual retreat,' or, 'I'm afraid I need Saturday to catch up,' both of which are rather lame. The best thing to do is, first, decide whether you are going to lie or not. Then, if you are, your soul is going to be in just as much peril for a big lie as for a little one, so you might as well let rip.

'Daphne, this is awful. I'm throwing a party myself. In fact, I was about to ring *you* to see whether you and Jock could come!'

This is an artful move, because an 'invite' counts for as much as an 'attendance', and since you now know she won't be able to come, you will have absolved yourself of any obligations for future dates. However, it could easily backfire.

'Sweetest! What a super piece of news. We'd love to come.'

'Oh! I thought –'

'Don't give it another thought, lovey. You were my first call anyway. We can fix our date for another time. Tell you what, let's do it now, so we make sure you two can come.'

Always arrive late at dinner parties. Make sure one of you is on the wagon – alcohol flows freely in country houses – and be sure to dress warmly, especially in summer, when there will be no fire in the drawing room. Dress often causes immense embarrassment because 'informal' can mean anything from a grubby sweater to a gownless evening strap. Phoning first to find out the form is no help because nobody wants to give the game away.

'Daphne? Sylvia here.'

'Hullo.'

'Darling, I know you must be horrendously busy but we just wondered what we ought to wear.'

'Whatever you like, loves.'

'Suits? Casual?'

'Whatever's your bag, really. It's you we love, not your clothes.'

'But what will Jock be wearing?'

'God knows! Casual, I expect.'

'Casual. Right. See you soon, darling. We're *so* looking forward. Byeee!'

When you arrive, in casual garb, Jock answers the door similarly attired in an open-necked shirt and slacks. You heave a sigh of relief, prematurely of course, because all the other guests are in dark suits or long skirts.

'My dears! Here you are at last!' whoops Daphne, emerging from the kitchen in a little black number by Givenchy. 'Jock, love, go and change out of those *awful* clothes. I can hold the fort now.'

Conversation at country dinner parties often drags, especially if you are used to functions where wit is rapid rather than vapid. Most topics are taboo. Sex is out, of course; so is art, literature, music and piles. Piles of money (other people's) is permissible and should be freely discussed, but the main topics are farming, shooting, farming, hunting and farming. After the cheese course, the ladies depart, leaving their men behind, and from that point the conversation changes to sex, farming, hunting, shooting and sex. Here is a typical country dinner party scenario.

The hosts are Jock and Daphne Shortcake, company director and dress-shop owner – his boutique is called 'Cuddly Clo's' and she runs an international firm of consultant engineers. They are entertaining Bruce and Hilda Thighroyd (cattle farmers), Tristan and Cynthia Brainewarp (arable farmers) and Norman and Anthea Wellington-Greene (land agents). We, the flies on the wall, have just buzzed in as they are getting down to their main course. All the 'Um – sorry, may I?', 'No, no, after you' and 'Ooh, sprouts, how I *adore* them,' as if they were a rare and special food on a par with beluga caviar, are over and the serious conversation is under way.

Bruce: How *are* your sprouts, by the way, Tris?

Tristan: Delicious, thanks. I love them lightly cooked.

Daphne: *Al dente*.

Bruce: Al who? Is that another of your operas or something?

Daphne: It means crunchy.

Bruce: Ah. Raw. [To Tristan] No, I meant how is your *crop* of sprouts?

Tristan: Fine. Picking's going quite well but there's a bit of mildew about.

Bruce: Can't you spray for that?

Tristan: Oh aah. But the *pathetic* Ministry regulations don't allow us to spray when the crop is ready for eating.

Hilda: Daphne, how *do* you manage to get your potatoes so deliciously crisp on the outside?

Daphne: Well, it's not that difficult really. You just . . .

Norman: [To Cynthia] Anyway, just as the beaters were coming out of the wood, a single high bird came over like an express train right between our two guns . . .

Cynthia: zzzz.

Jock: [To Anthea] No, much as Daphne loves music and things, she's perfectly happy here. She just gets a little bored from time to time because it's a three-hour drive to the National Theatre or Covent Garden.

Anthea: Oh, I wouldn't send produce to Covent Garden if I were you. The pricing's far too capricious. Most of the growers round here market through the local cooperatives.

Jock: Ah. I really meant –

Anthea: You'll have to get her interested in a few local activities. Does she ride?

Jock: No. She was bitten by a horse when she was four and has been terrified of them ever since.

Anthea: Sensible girl. What about shooting?

Jock: Hardly. She abhors guns of all kinds.

Anthea: Oh dear. Well, what about Oxfam or Meals on Wheels?

Jock: I don't think she'd have time. You see, she works a sixteen-hour day and quite often at weekends too. The business she runs is quite large.

Anthea: Really? Norman manages to fit in plenty of shooting and go'f even though Humm, Rutt and Strutter are pretty big land agents. I mean his job is very demanding too.

Norman: [Still to Cynthia] Anyway, the minute lunch was over we went back to the far side of the spinney but the east wind was so strong by then that all the birds were flying low and to the right of the guns . . .

Cynthia: z z z z z z.

Daphne: Norman, what else do you like doing?

Norman: Deer stalking's fun. Duck can be worthwhile, down on the washes, when they come flighting in high on a frosty evening – about four o'clock, just before dark. You need to put a knob of clay on your gun sights so –

Hilda: I think Daphne meant other than shooting.

Norman: Oh. [Falls silent]

Hilda: We're going to London next week, for Smithfield. And we're going to the Opera.

Daphne: Good for you. How lovely.

Hilda: Well, after what you said last time, I thought we'd be a bit adventurous this year. So instead of the Farmers' Club Dinner, we're going to the Opera.

Daphne: My dear, you'll love it! What are you going to see? *Figaro*'s on at the Garden and the ENO are doing a fabulous production of *Peter Grimes*.

Hilda: I told you. Opera. *Phantom of the Opera*. You know, that Lloyd-Loom thing.

Daphne: Ah.

Friends and Neighbours

When you burst a pipe or lose a roof, country neighbours are precious beings. At other times they can be pesky. The cup-of-sugar situation seldom arises with large country houses because by the time you've done a half-mile jog to the nearest dwelling and back again, all the sugar will have jumped out of the cup or gone soggy in the rain. Nevertheless, there has to be a high degree of interdependence in sparsely populated communities.

Neighbouring farmers are usually harmless, but their animals can be problematic. A prize Jersey bull, if it breaks out of the neighbouring field and takes possession of your tennis court, will not leave until it has ruined the grass, trampled the flower beds and charged everyone and everything in sight, including your favourite apple tree, which it fells with a single head-butt. Ditto that rather expensive statue you had placed as a vista stop. Naturally, its head breaks off – the statue's, not the bull's – on impact and this so disturbs him that he charges off in the opposite direction and falls into the swimming pool. Another interesting agricultural fact is that ruminants – animals like cattle – which have complicated digestive systems designed to convert low-grade fodder into meat and milk, are capable of developing a really serious tummy upset in a staggeringly short time. Thus a cowpat, at times of stress, becomes a cow deluge. What you fetch up with in your beautiful garden is a sea of wreckage decorated with copious amounts of bull!

Sheep, though smaller, come in greater numbers. They have an inborn need to break out and, having formed their own escape committee in the neighbouring field, will organise for one of their flock to hold up the wire of the fence while all the others come through into the garden. Once they are in, panic arises because they dislike their new surroundings and have lost the security of their field. In the resulting stampede, the whole fence gets obliterated. Then comes the painful telephone confrontation with your neighbour, the farmer.

'Hullo, could I speak to Mr Mangold.'

'Yes.'

'Thanks.'

Long silence, wheezy breathing at the other end, then: 'Yes?'

'You said I could speak to Mr Mangold.'

'You are.'

'Oh. It's about your sheep.'

'What about 'em?'

'They're in my garden.'

'What, again?'

''fraid so. They've eaten my herbaceous border and ruined the lawn.'

'Not my fault.'

'I wondered if you could do something about them.'

'Doubt it. You keep encouraging them.'

'I what?'

'You keep tempting 'em. All them flowers and stuff. Entices 'em.'

'But your fence is wrecked. They can just walk in whenever they want now.'

'Ah. I was going to talk to you about that. How about some compensation.'

'Oh, well, that will help, I suppose. It won't bring the flowers back this year but it would help pay for some new plants for next season.'

'Yer what? No, I mean how about you compensating us for fence damage.'

'For the fence *your* sheep damaged?'

'Like I said. You tempted 'em. They trampled the fence to get to yer flarze.'

'Actually, they didn't do much damage to the fence coming in. It was when they went out again.'

'Proves my point. Yer must have scared 'em. It'll cost you more than just the fence.'

'What?'

'Yer'll 'ave run some of the fat off them. I'll need compensation for that too.'

A seasoned rural dweller would know how to handle this. He would have steered things thus.

'I absolutely agree with you, Mr Mangold. Would you care to consider your costs and name a figure?'

'I'll name one now, if yer like. I know my costs all right.'

'Well?'

''undred quid in cash or 'hundred 'n' fifty cheque.'

'Fine. That seems reasonable. Good bye.'

Then, after a week or two, he will send a note to Mangold which says:

Dear Mr Mangold

To compensation for fence damage and running of fat off your sheep, £100 as agreed.

Damage to my lawn, £75.00; cost of new plant material for mixed border, £78.49; and loss of enjoyment and benefit from current season's plants, £50. Net owing to me, £103.49. I'd settle for £100 if you paid promptly.

Yours, etc.

He'll settle, of course, but for him prompt payment means within twenty-four calendar months.

By now you should have a reasonable idea of how to integrate into the rural community. Try these exercises, just to make sure.

1 In England a man is allowed to own whatever gun he likes and can shoot game anywhere, within reason, without the landowner's permission. True or false?

2 The best way to learn the ways of *genuine* country folk is to:
(a) Read Thomas Hardy, **(b)** sleep in a ditch for a month, **(c)** take out a subscription to *Country Living*, **(d)** be born and bred out of hearing of Bow Bells.

3 How would you address the following rural craftsmen?
(a) Warrener, **(b)** eel bobber, **(c)** reddleman, **(d)** artificial inseminator.

4 What is the difference between a professional farmer and someone who just does it for fun?

Answers

1 False, mostly, but true in France.

2 None of these. There are no genuine country folk, not even in Ambridge.

3 Any way you like, although 'Wotcher cock!' might be a shade tactless for the last one.

4 A fortnight. Think about that. If you savvy, you are really coming on. Well done you! If you're mystified, start househunting – in Greater London.

Chapter 5

Coping with Red Tape

It is obvious that there are certain interferences with personal freedom . . .

(From L. W. White and W. D. Hussey, *Government*, 2nd edn, Cambridge University Press, 1958)

Birmingham New Street Station, Platform 12a. The outside temperature is 1° below freezing. The 17.41 to Cambridge is standing at the platform, cleaned, serviced and ready for use. It is not due to leave for thirty minutes but there are already a dozen or so passengers stamping their feet and flapping their arms, trying to get warm. The train doors are shut but the lights shining through the windows make the carriages look warm and cosy compared to the chill twilight outside. One passenger, bolder than the rest, tries to open a door to board the train. A railway man appears from nowhere.

'Hoi!' he shouts. 'You keep off!'

'Can't we get on?' pleads the passenger. 'We're all freezing.'

'You came too early, mate! You can't get on until ten minutes before departure. That's the rules.'

The good thing about having rules and regulations, as any sociologist will tell you, is that they stop people from riding rough-shod over each other. The bad thing about them is that people who make the rules, and those who are employed to enforce them, think that they exist for their own personal pleasure.

Politicians play the role of lawmakers but in reality have no power at all. The people who *really* make the rules are top civil servants. This desire to order other people about for the fun of it starts at school. Because their mothers and fathers think private education away from home is better, our embryonic leaders are sent off to freezing cold prep schools in the country, where they are fed a diet of Latin, cold lumpy porage (or porridge) and bullying. Just before puberty, when they are at their most vulnerable, they are thrown out of this environment into one of Britain's top ten public schools. Here, the bullying continues and, in addition, they have to learn hundreds of meaningless rules and orders. 'Boys below "Remove A" must wear a cricket bat down the inside of their left trouser legs at all times' or 'All masters' ladies must be greeted with the words "*Salve uxor magistri, ego vermis sum*" ' is the sort of thing they are up against. By the time they reach 'A' level, a proportion of these youngsters will have become so twisted inside and, at the same time, so obsessed with legislation that as long as they can get into Oxford or Cambridge, they will become top civil servants.

While they are up at university, they will probably be recruited into the secret service as well. It doesn't really matter whose they join, ours or theirs, as long as they are able to live out their lives giving legislation lunatic interpretations, overlooking wise judgements but homing in like bloodhounds on every dubious decision any dotty old judge well into his second childhood ever made. To survive in the country, you need to know how to live with the effects such legislators cause. Rural communities are not very heavily represented and often bear the brunt of bad decisions made in the comfort of Whitehall or the county offices.

Planning

The first difficult laws you encounter will almost certainly have to do with planning. If you live in a listed building, whatever you want to do to it will be made problematic by laws regarding listed buildings. If your village is in a conservation area, things will be even more awkward because nobody is allowed to touch anything.

Imagine buying a derelict, sixteenth-century cottage in the middle of a conservation village. You intend to renovate the building, making it fit for human habitation, but the first thing you long to get to grips with is that repulsive corrugated-iron lean-to on the west elevation. Gleefully, you brandish your sledgehammer but, ere you take the first swing, a person in military tweeds and a trilby hat trots up the street towards your cottage. On closer examination you discover that, in spite of the moustache, it's a woman.

'Excuse me, young man,' she says imperiously, a little out of breath from trotting, the large tweedy bosom heaving rather. 'I hope you're not going to do anything unwise.'

'Hullo. I don't think we've met. My name's Colborn.'

'Oh. Oh, yes. How rude of me. Brenda Hardcastle. I'm chairman of the Piddle-on-the-Wold Conservation Society. Did you say Cockburn? Anything to do with the port?'

'Wrong spelling, I'm afraid.'

'Oh, I see. Well, what are you doing with that sledgehammer?'

'Thought I'd do away with this eyesore.'

'What. Goodness gracious! You can't do that!'

'Why not? It's nearly fallen down of its own accord anyway.'

'Nonsense, it's as sound as a bell. Outbuildings are part of the conservation area too, you know. You can't just go ruining our heritage any time you feel like it.'

'Heritage? This grotty old tin lean-to? It's because of the heritage I want to get rid of it. So I can improve the cottage.'

'Improve? I don't like the sound of that young man. It's not for you to decide. Somebody pulled down an Elizabethan cow byre a few years ago, but we made him put it all back.'

'I don't think this corrugated iron is exactly Elizabethan, do you?'

'That is for the experts to decide. Meanwhile, I must warn you that any attempt to demolish it, or any other part of this cottage, will meet with our stern disapproval. You must learn the procedure in these matters, young man. Submit your plans and we will decide what is acceptable and what isn't. Good day to you.'

As you watch her retreating figure, a character in a woolly hat, sweater and low-cut jeans approaches. The splashes of plaster and paint on the jeans, not to mention the exposed buttocks, tells you that he is a builder.

'Wotcher, mate. 'avin' trouble wiv the Merry Widow?'

'I beg your pardon?'

''swhat we call 'er. I'm convertin' them barns over the street there. Right thorn in our side she's been.'

'Ah. Well, I don't want to tread on anyone's toes, but I would rather like to get rid of this repulsive tin shed. She says I mustn't.'

'Silly old cow. Still, she's right. Technically you ain't supposed to demolish nothink.'

'But I'm dying to get started.'

'Have an accident, then. Drive something into it. Doesn't look as though it'll take much pushing over.'

'Drive what into it?'

'Well, a tractor or something.'

'But I've only got a Fiat Uno.'

'Oh blimey! Tell you wot. Slip me a tenner an' I'll get Bert ter park 'is JCB there ternight. It'll only take a nudge with the bucket – accidental, like.'

'Well, if you're sure.'

'Just leave it ter the experts, Sunshine. When yer come back termorrer, it'll be gorn. Er, don't forgit the tenner, mate.'

When you return to Piddle-on-the-Wold next morning the shed has indeed gorn. It's lying flattened under the heap of red brick rubble that used to be the western wall of your sixteenth-century cottage.

Everyone in the country recognises the need for more housing. Nobody wants any of it in their village. Born Countrymen, especially farmers, are only really interested in getting planning permission on their own fields. When a paddock without planning sells at about £1,800 an acre and one with sells at half a million, you can see the motivation. Rustic workers seldom mind either way, especially now that they've all bought their own council houses, but émigré rural dwellers are fanatics. Put up as much as an unscheduled window box and they'll be on to you in a body, especially if you plant it with salvias and French marigolds. The fact that most incomers live in new housing, or in converted buildings, is quite irrelevant to their views. Once they have got

'Just leave it ter the experts, Sunshine.'

their own feet under the table they're blowed if anyone else is going to be allowed to wreck the environment.

Because few natives take much interest in parish meetings or community affairs, the outsiders reign supreme, imposing their values on the community regardless of what might be best for everyone. A garage or filling station, for instance, could help to keep a village alive, providing employment for several inhabitants and offering a useful service. (Have you thought what rural life might be like without a car? Impossible!) But filling stations are nasty, ugly things which don't belong in the country, so they are blocked and prevented.

How to get Planning Permission

There is no formula! Everything depends on a system of old-boy networks, making sure the *right* people get invited to a day's shooting, and, of course, blackmail. The simple procedures which follow *might* help you to succeed with your application, but don't be too hopeful.

1 Find out who is chairman of your local planning committee. Make sure that: (a) you get to know all about him, (b) you convince him that it is definitely in his interest to be kind to you, (c) he understands that you are the right sort of person to associate with, and (d) you have tried to find out any flaws he may have in his character – sexual peccadilloes, a secret alcohol problem, an inability to pronounce the word 'dais', that sort of thing – so that you can use them as a lever.

2 Make sure the architect you retain is in cahoots with all the planning officers.

3 Make your proposals look as though they are going to be of vast benefit to the village or to mankind. For instance, if you want to build a large house with swimming pool and triple garage on the village green, put in an application for a convent which will educate physically handicapped children. You can always change the use after the first application has been approved.

4 Never, never utter the words 'green belt', 'tree felling' or

'executive housing'. Rather, say 'infill', 'starter homes', 'sympathetic conversion' and 'in keeping' – they have much better vibes.

Forgive us our Trespasses

The sign which says 'Trespassers Will Be Prosecuted', unless you happen to be part of a hippie convoy going to Stonehenge, means very little. Strolling through somebody else's woods is not trespassing; picnicking in their meadows or swimming in their river is not trespassing. Shooting their pheasants or netting their salmon is trespassing, and it's also poaching, which is criminal. So what is trespass? How should I know, I'm not a lawyer, but doing damage to land and property is certainly unlawful. Suppose, as a complete stranger, you enter a private garden uninvited. As the family are settling down to afternoon tea on the terrace, you tip granny off the patio lounger, grab teapot, cup, plate and cut yourself a Billy-Bunter-style slice of fruitcake. Could this be called trespass or is it just bloody rude? It depends where you are. In Wimbledon, offence would probably be taken, but why not try it in deepest Gloucestershire? See how you get on.

Open countryside needs to be more accessible, we are told, so you should do your bit for the cause by walking over as many fields as possible and by frequenting all woodland, especially in spring, when the breeding pheasants are easily disturbed. Be sure to discuss cropping techniques with local farmers and don't be afraid to hold up their work for a bit of Archers-style gossip – they love it. Never ask a farmer whether you can enter his domain. He will always welcome you and will not expect you to bother to seek permission. When walking through fruit and vegetable crops, take a basket or plastic bag, as squashed fruit can stain the pockets.

Preventing trespass from being done unto you is not so easy. You can use reasonable force to eject intruders, but what is 'reasonable force'? Waving a twelve-bore in their faces or setting the Lhasa Apso on them is unreasonable. Booting their behinds is called 'assault'; indeed, any physical contact could be called assault, so 'reasonable force' means inviting them to leave. They don't always go!

Supposing it is September and you are just off to your private paddock because you know the hedges are thick with luscious blackberries and there are hundreds of large mushrooms growing in the grass. You arrive in time to find a family of seven laden with baskets, not only of mushrooms and blackberries but also of sloes and wild hazelnuts. Legally, you could demand that they hand the lot over to you, but dare you? There are so many of them and the elder sons look like Arnold Schwarzenegger only stronger. And could you, in all conscience, confiscate their loot when they have obviously been working hard all day? After all, they're wild fruit, so it's finders keepers really, isn't it?

Putting up threatening notices has no effect on the public at all. They believe they have natural right of access to all fields, woodland and water, but resorting to misinformation can help. A noticeboard reading 'Caution – Minefield' might stretch people's credibility, but 'Danger – Quicksands' is convincing in the right terrain. 'Beware of Adders' works quite well, except that enthusiastic herpetologists are likely to come flocking. Baffling would-be trespassers with science can succeed. How about a notice saying 'Agropyron Repens at Large' or 'Warning – Designated Cocksfoot Area'?

Nimby Policy

Whenever a serious threat arises near your village, everyone will pull together to prevent the worst from happening – or will they? Our village, at the end of a no-through road, is separated from most of Britain by the London–Edinburgh railway. When British Rail decided to go electric, at a stroke turning Peterborough, Grantham, Doncaster and York into London suburbs, all the bridges alone the line had to be demolished and rebuilt. The first to be replaced in our parish carried a cart track joining fields and was used by one of the local farmers. A temporary Bailey bridge was installed for the farmer, so that his freedom to cross the railway was uninterrupted until the permanent bridge had been completed, at a cost of £240,000. But when the time came for our main village bridge to be rebuilt, British Rail applied for road closure for three months, meaning half the parishioners had a six-mile diversion to go to the post office or phone box. There was consternation and I started a protest group. Initial support was overwhelming; at a special meeting called to discuss the problem, five people showed up.

Not deterred, I phoned the highway authority, who told me I had no business to know who or what had applied for closure and that as ours was a B road carrying little traffic, I was to mind my own business and let them get on with running the highways. Several letters, including one from our MP, bless him, got to British Rail and I phoned the official concerned and advised him that there would be a sit-in across the old bridge, preventing the bulldozers from starting. I didn't elaborate on likely numbers, airily suggesting that the whole community was up in arms, knowing that if it came to a real protest, the sit-in would probably consist of me and the family Labrador. British Rail backed down and withdrew their application. Indeed, they had applied merely as a matter of routine and had been staggered to receive a go-ahead from the highway authority in the first place.

The moral is, when an eyesore is threatened, start your own protest group. Even if very few of you actually do anything about preventing the undesired motorway, gravel pit or sewage works, you must create the impression that a vast army of crusaders is ready to march on Whitehall at a moment's notice.

Minor Nuisance

Within a very short time of moving into the country, you will discover several painful truths. Chief of these is that farming must be allowed to go on in whatever way the farmer pleases, regardless of nuisance. From July until October, narrow lanes carry convoys of gigantic combine harvesters moving at top speed – nine mph –

and always choosing the busiest time of the day to move. After harvest, the combines are replaced by monstrous four-wheel-drive tractors with double wheels which distribute mud evenly along the road surface for miles. At winter's end, helicopters start dropping ammonium nitrate on to crops in ground too sodden for tractors to pass through. Later, the same aircraft spray insecticide on to oilseed rape crops to kill the pollen beetles and other insect pests, not to mention bees, butterflies, birds and cyclists.

One of the chief ingredients of agriculture is noise. Tractors roar, combines roar, feed mills hum, elevators rattle and livestock bellow or squeal. Try listening to lambs which have been weaned and separated from their mums, or pigs being moved. But the most spine-chilling sound of all, ominous because of what it signifies as well as its murderously amplified buzzing, is the chainsaw. Most farmers operate them between two pm and dusk on Sundays. Just how many trees can be felled by two chainsaws in an afternoon has to be seen to be believed. The irony is that most of these are logged and sold to new country dwellers for their log fires and woodstoves. Natives burn coal or have oil-fired central heating.

Any non-agricultural industry which makes noise in the country is intolerable, but farmers should be allowed to make as much din as they like. Combining or ploughing may continue for twenty-four hours a day at busy times, so if you are bordered by open country, expect a few restless nights in late summer. Anyone who tries to prevent a farmer from making noise at dead of night simply doesn't understand the food needs of the nation and should be banished. The farmer, on the other hand, will be among the first to complain about non-agricultural nuisance. His straw burning is a necessary activity, even if it threatens your thatch and fills your house with smuts. Your barbecue, on the other hand, is a frivolous activity which puts his neighbouring cornfields at unnecessary risk. His combining may, legitimately, mar your Sunday afternoon's peace, but your kids' ghetto blaster, if it disturbs his partridges, will result in instant prosecution – and he's probably the local JP to boot. You don't stand a chance.

Trees and TPOs

To native country people, trees exist to be felled. When first we clapped eyes on the crumbling manor which became our home, one of the most impressive features was a vast lime tree. Majestically, it towered over the piles of scrap metal, elder scrub and corrugated-iron sheds which constituted the garden. 'Of course,' said a helpful neighbour, 'you'll be wanting that old tree down. I can see to it for you.' We were horrified.

'Don't you dare,' I said. 'It's magnificent.'

'Gerttcha! 's'neither use nor ornament!'

But we kept it, of course, and it now presides over the garden, making a wonderful focal point. The only person to have criticised its presence since was a qualified landscape architect, who thought it 'out of proportion'. To guard against any such nonsense, in the event of our dying or moving out, a Tree Preservation Order has been placed on it.

In our village there are, not counting our lime, roughly a dozen outstanding specimens, including a vast fern-leaved beech, a giant redwood and a fine Turkey oak. Most of them grow in one garden, where their lives are precarious because they are not protected by preservation orders. Some years ago, I managed to rescue them from the chainsaw of a new young gardener simply by telling lies. He was a fascistic young man whose mind seemed constantly to hover between sex and death. In between frenzied efforts to impregnate the nanny in the potting shed, he used to come over to our farm and volunteer to kill some of our capons. The glint in his eye was matched only by the gloss of his weapon – a huge hunting knife. His employers were away at the time of the chainsaw incident but had succumbed to his plea to 'remove some of the rubbish' to let more light into the garden. I managed to persuade him that the owners had bought the rectory mainly because of the grandeur of the trees and that they knew every one by name, so if he valued his new job, he'd leave them be.

Far from serving the interests of the trees themselves, TPOs are more commonly used as a form of aggression. Suppose the landowner wants to build on a roadside site. There may be a scrubby poplar tree there or perhaps a few seedling sycamores. Get a TPO on these and the planning application is squashed.

Well, goodness me, that's quite enough whingeing about red tape. Here are some exercises.

1 For which of the following activities do you need Listed Building Consent?
(a) Changing the window frames, **(b)** changing the door furniture, **(c)** changing the curtains.

2 Which of the following activities are illegal?
(a) Burning a field of straw on Sunday, **(b)** shooting someone's pet dog without provocation, **(c)** felling other people's hedgerow timber, **(d)** putting poison sprays into the village stream.

3 How would you block a planning application for a farmer to erect a 60 x 40 foot galvanised tin shed to house five combine harvesters, a potato lifter and four tractors in the meadow between the village and its thirteenth-century church?

Answers

1 All of these.

2 All of them, but you'd be amazed at how often farmers do them and get away with it.

3 You couldn't. Planning consent would not be needed.

Chapter 6

My Dear, You Should See Her Interiors

What a dump!

(Martha in Edward Albee's, *Who's Afraid of Virginia Woolf?*)

The way we speak tends to classify us, but not half so much as the way we decorate our homes. In these days of elocution lessons and smile school, few people can guess at the kind of background a person may have had, but step through their front doors and within seconds you will have seen several dead giveaways.

The more obvious signs can be dispensed with fairly swiftly. An oar with nine names written in gold on the blade suggests not just a sporty background but that there's a fair chance the owner was at a university on a river. Yacht pictures indicate a sailing fanatic and a bit and bridle hanging in the scullery might lead you to think either that a rider lived there or else that the family was into some extremely peculiar perversions. But what about the subtle signs? The way curtains are hung, the way flowers and plants are arranged, wallpaper types and colours, how the children's bedrooms look, what goes on in the kitchen and, above all, what the furniture is like.

You may find your move to the country coincides with a change in your persona and therefore you will want to revise the way in which you arrange the innards of your house. The purpose of this chapter is to look at some of the alternatives and help you to make your choice.

Kitchen

In all houses the kitchen is the heart. It's where divorce is seeded, where culinary triumphs and disasters are made, where most serious floods begin and frequently where householders die. Before going into details about the perfect country kitchen, let's look at some of the items which do so much to give away the innermost secrets about a person's make-up.

They are listed in three categories:

1 Excellent items – not necessarily taste-wise, but the sort of thing a really sensible and practical rural family might have.

2 Not quite so desirable – in fact, a bit naff really, but not beyond the pale.

3 Unspeakable – objects which are pretentious, ugly or just plain silly.

Excellent items all houses need

Double sink – sensible size, none of your pathetic little rounded things which hold less than a pint.

Dog nest – preferably not sicked in, but if sicked in, at least turned over.

Capacious cooker – big enough to roast baron of lamb.

Fridge – big enough to hold half a pig.

Fruitbowl with wrinkled apples and spotted bananas.

Hoover – doubles as modern sculpture in corner when not in use.

Table to seat at least eight – sturdy enough to butcher a lamb on or to use as a flamenco stage.

Useful cupboards – roomy with plenty of shelves and strong hinges.

Dishwasher – strong enough to handle calf buckets, goat's cheese equipment and teat cups.

Hooks for strings of garlic, aprons, gardening hats, dead pheasants, etc.

Scrubbable floor.

Shelf for heaping cookbooks.

Sensible pictures which go with the decor – preferably abstracts so the ketchup stains will blend in.

Not so good but forgivable

Food blender with all the extras.

Kniferack on wall.

Sophisticated coffeemaker – but not mother in the corner going 'glub, glub'!

Graded tins marked 'Flour', 'Sugar', etc.

Joke teacloth pinned to wall.

Child's first drawings, unless child is still under five.

Shopping-list holder.

Microwave.

Noticeboard with neat, legible messages on it.

Overhead drying rack which can be lowered on pulleys.

Toaster – but not with poppy or wheat design on its sides.

Large, earthenware crocks holding bread, salt, etc.

Dog bed on legs with curtain round.

Cat flap.

String baskets with ivies trailing from them.

Unspeakable

Pasta in long glass jars.

Net cloth or doyley over table.

Prints of vintage cars.

Chopping boards with pictures of food on them, hung up for show rather than used.

Frilly curtains.

Crowds of dried flowers hung up to dry six years before on drying rack with pulley (*see* Forgivable).

Kitchen carpeting.

Fake pine Welsh dressers.

Pot Toby jugs.

Water jugs shaped like fish which gurgle as you pour.

Wine bottles suspended over optics.

Frilly aprons which are useless but look pretty.

Tea cosy with hole for spout.

Plastic aprons with bosoms or suspender belts painted on them. Placards with joke rule sets or unfunny mottoes: 'You don't have to be mad to work here, but it helps', etc.

Since fitting out your kitchen is going to cost you at least £20,000, you might as well give it some careful thought. There are specialist firms which advise on design and layout, but you must remember that the people who design your kitchen don't actually have to use it. You do. In magazines, the interiors of kitchens always look as though nobody ever has or ever will be able to do more than boil an egg or shred a lettuce leaf because they seem to be arranged in such an impractical way. Do you really want to cross the room from sink to cooker every time you lift a saucepan or get something out of the oven? Does it help to have the cooking area in a sort of island in the middle, surrounded by a sea of space separating the hotplates from all the cupboards by the maximum distance?

The whole kitchen industry has grown up on swank. Cookers and fridges are not designed for efficiency but for looks. While men drool over elegant BMWs or Ferraris, women, we are told, dream of having the perfect Smallpiece kitchen or yearn to install the latest designs from Polpot. The only way such firms can keep on selling new kitchens is by changing fashions, so as soon as the paint has dried on one £20,000 creation, the trend changes from natural wood doors and soft-feel tops to plastic doors and tile tops, so the whole lot has to be ripped out. Prospective buyers viewing the house are bound to be deeply impressed with the kitchen if it looks expensive and may base their purchasing decision on that fact alone.

'Do come into the kitchen. We had it installed last May.'

'Oh my goodness, it's *lovely*. I adore the sink unit. How clever to have the taps concealed under a lid like that. Who designed it?'

'Hottentot. They sent their own expert. So convenient like that. All we had to do was approve the drawings.'

'I *love* the cupboard doors. Is that real timber?'

'Oh yes. Norfolk Island pine with musclewood trim.'

'Positively sumptuous. Don't you think so, Gerald? It must have cost a fortune.'

'It did rather.'

'And I adore the cooking arrangements. How brilliant to have installed the flush hob just there. Your man must have been awfully clever. And the ovens – simply perfect. And I *adore* the colours. Makes you feel inspired to great culinary feats. I bet you're a superb cook.'

'Well, one tries.'

Later, as she and Gerald are going home, he asks:

'Well, what do you think?'

'It's a pretty house, very pretty, but, Gerald, that *ghastly* kitchen!'

'I thought you liked it?'

'Oh, darling, come on! That repulsive yellow wallpaper and ludicrous little sink.'

'It could be changed.'

'It'd cost a mint. All those poky little cupboards would have to go. That assinine tap cover would drive you nuts. As for the cooker.'

'What's wrong with the cooker?'

'Nothing. It's where it is. Well, come to that, it's where everything is. So inconvenient. I don't know how she manages. You couldn't slice a kiwi in there without having to do about fifty unnecessary movements. No, we'd have to do a complete rethink there. Pretty house though.'

In country kitchens, you need space. You will be buying whole lambs, sides of beef or half pigs. These need cutting up to freeze, *ergo* you need a large, sturdy kitchen table – not to mention a strong arm. You may have acquired a goat or a house cow, in which case you'll need to spread dairy equipment about. If you go shooting, you will want to eviscerate your pheasants and hares and be able to wash down the walls afterwards, so you'll need a strong stomach as well as a strong arm. Furthermore, flock wallpaper won't wash down very easily. London is about the only place in England where one can buy truly fresh fruit and vegetables. In the country, you have to choose between eating stale, frozen or canned produce and growing your own. One aspect of self-sufficiency is that 93 per cent of the fruit and vegetables reach maturity in the third week in July. Thus, you will have several weeks of frantic blanching, peeling, chopping, slicing and freezing, or, if you are old fashioned enough, bottling and jamming. During summer, that kitchen will become a food-processing factory. There simply isn't room for pretty, frilly things or little arrangements of air-dried rosebuds.

Lavatory

After reading the last section, you'll probably need the loo, so we'll go into this room next. The smallest room, usually, but it gives so much away. We'll also be considering bathrooms in this section.

Desirable
Functional seat and pan.
Proper flush designed to handle heavy loads.
White basin, bath, lavatory, etc.
Shower.
Pictures of hunting scenes or amusing newspaper cuttings.
Decent-sized towels.

Borderline
Bidet.
Magazines within reach of lavatory, but only the *Spectator* or *Country Life* – absolutely nothing pornographic.
Pot plant.
Cork-seated chair.
Telephone.

Unspeakable
Pictures which are slightly rude in a twee way: French dogs sniffing, little boys urinating into pots, back views of sailors peeing into harbours and comparing endowments – awful stuff like that.
Signs on the door saying 'Toilet', 'yer 'tis', or 'The Smallest Room'.
Lavatory-seat covers.

Objects which turn the water into blue ink every time the cistern flushes, making you think you've got some dire kidney disease.
Coloured basin, bath, etc.
Shag-pile carpet.
Jacuzzi.
Hotel soaps from exotic places – place dropping.
Dried flowers.

Piles of magazines in lavatories suggest either that the owners have constipation or that they went to a public school. As anyone at boarding school knows, the bogs are the only places where absolute privacy is guaranteed, and for many youngsters the daily visit became a cherished period of quiet solitude. My own view is that there is something rather unhygienic about the idea of shuffling pages in that place and one should either perform or get off the pot.

Most glossy magazines show interiors with bathrooms which are even more impractical than the kitchens. There may be festoons of tropical foliage, all thriving in the humid climate, through which one has to hack one's way to get to the water works. Baths, nowadays, are often placed in the middle of the room, surrounded on all sides by rickety tables on which stand porcelain putti, dishes holding about 800 bars of soap, vases of dried flowers – just to keep up the illusion of tropical forest – and rank on rank of bottles containing jojoba (pronounced hchhohchhoba!) oil, sandalwood bath balm, asses' milk and 3 in 1. One false move and the whole lot can come crashing into the bath with you. Break into a snatch from *Die Meistersinger* and you are relatively safe, but start conducting and suddenly you're sitting on broken glass.

Then there is the dreaded Jacuzzi. There is something rather sexy about a Jacuzzi. The thought of all that warm water pummelling and bubbling about your nether regions, you would think, is sure to be nice. But all a Jacuzzi does is to let you know what a saucepan of King Edwards feels like just before Sunday lunch.

Bedrooms

Bedrooms are private places. We outsiders would not be welcome under normal circumstances. However, these days they are beginning to be used as showplaces. Go upstairs during a dinner party and, more often than not, the bedroom doors will be open, inviting one to take a crafty peep. The exceptions are children's bedrooms. These are strictly private and they're inclined to lower the tone anyway, so that a discerning hostess will want to shut and lock the kids' doors during social functions.

A child's room, if you are able to glimpse one, says much about the family. The spoilt brat, for instance, sleeps in a cushioned environment. Mummy (or Nanny) makes his bed every day and all his toys are neatly stowed on shelves. Clothes are hung up, again by his mother, and there is television, hi-fi and video all of his very own. When he was very young, he slept in a little bed shaped like Noddy's car, but later, when he lost his fix on Big Ears, he was given a proper bed, done out in royal blue gloss paint with Biggles transfers. He collects videos and makes plastic model aircraft – every one a perfectly painted replica of the real thing. These are arranged on the otherwise empty bookshelves. When he goes to Charterhouse next term, Nanny will have to dust them every day. He has a home computer but plays only games on it and his chief aim in life is to grow up and have a Porsche like Daddy's.

His sister has muslin bedcovers covered with little pink rosebuds. She has a pony, even though she's only eleven, and tries to get to all the gymkhanas. Her room is decorated in strawberry pink and white shades, so that being there feels like sitting inside a valentine card. She has a collection of books about ponies and a mountain of cuddly toys.

The ordinary boy's bedroom is an unspeakable tip. He has drawings of the major star constellations stuck to his ceiling with sticky tape. In places this has peeled the paint. His wardrobe is too full of *Dr Who* books to be able to hold any clothes, so his best suit is screwed up under the bed, alongside his school uniform, one shoe, a couple of apple cores and the remains of his brother's model spaceship. He collects fossils, so his chest of drawers has tripled its weight because of the rocks on its top. Once his walls had bright emulsion paint all over them, but now they are covered with posters of astronauts walking on the moon, cinema posters of Humphrey Bogart, his school timetable, Mendeleef's *Periodic Table of Elements*, splodges of ink and something that looks like dried coffee but is best not investigated more closely. His bookcase groans with copies of textbooks on astronomy, palaeontology, aviation, wildlife and fictional works by Roald Dahl and Penelope Lively (read) and Kipling, Sapper and Mark Twain (unread).

The native country boy's room will be a variation on this theme. He will have a .410 shotgun in the wardrobe and various horrendous specimens of stuffed birds or animals dotted about. Since he's doing his own taxidermy, these will smell awful. The fossils may not be there, but there will be aquaria full of leeches, tadpoles, sticklebacks and other pond life. Worse by far, because the contents of aquaria tend to stay put or perish, will be his vivarium, where the snakes live. Snakes and lizards are active and crafty, escaping frequently and surprising other members of the family by appearing from behind cushions in the drawing room at inopportune moments. In our household, we never suffered snakes, but I can still remember the bloodcurdling scream from a temporary home help who closed the hall curtains and found herself staring into the malevolent eyes of a giant stick insect.

Country girls' rooms are different but equally chaotic. There may be a selection of healthy plants on the windowsill, but it will be difficult to see them because of the festoons of tights hung up to get the damp out of them. The floor is littered with abandoned pieces of crochet work, knitting, sewing and tapestries which have been begun but are unlikely to get much further. On the walls are posters of Jeremy Irons, pop stars, including one stunted individual whose face is so ravaged by plastic surgery that he (she?) can adopt only a frozen mask which approximates a smile, and an obese hairy television wildlife presenter whose manufactured plebeian accent seems to grate on the ears even as he leers out of the silent poster.

In any house the master bedroom can be designed either for comfort or for show. The two don't go together. If you plan to have your finished country residence featured in *Country Living*, you'll have to go for the latter. In which case your bed needs to be on a dais surrounded by festoons of lace and net, so that it looks like a giant wedding dress. The usual wobbly tables, top heavy with dried flowers and dangerously balanced ornaments, need to be placed strategically, and rather than carpet, there should be polished tiles or ancient oak floorboards, smoothed by centuries of passing feet – and a few hours with the electric polishing machine. Other bedroom furniture should be minimal but should still suggest clutter. An old American-style rocking chair, perhaps, or even a genuine spinning wheel. Among these rustic bibelots you'll need to sprinkle a handful of modern gadgets essential for the *right* kind of lifestyle. A rowing machine perhaps, or a bicycle that goes nowhere.

Rooms designed for comfort are not difficult to imagine for town houses, but the country house produces special needs. The bed will want at least one extra duvet, because as soon as the heating goes off at night the temperature drops to freezing. Pipes can freeze and burst in the night, so a place is needed for wellingtons and overcoat – unless you've had the foresight to lag the pipes. Bedside glasses of water freeze too, unless lagged.

Night time is when all the rodents come out to play and when they have finished emptying the contents from the mouse-proof containers in the kitchen, they will come upstairs to scamper about the bedrooms, so you need to set traps. Sensitive souls will also need earplugs, because there is nothing more sinister than the sound of scurrying mousy feet, a loud snap and then silence. That's the point when you forget the havoc they've wreaked in the pantry and can remember only their dear little wuffly noses and bright, boot-button eyes.

Owning a cat might be a useful alternative, because it could keep you warm in bed and also catch mice. I suppose in theory you could use mice to warm the bed, but you'd need an awful lot of them and they are inclined to nibble holes in the bedding.

In large country houses, you soon learn that the warmest place is bed, so it pays to lay on radio, television and videos which can be operated from within the bed. Fitted carpet is absolutely essential and a bathroom *en suite* a near necessity, because a

Owning a cat might be a useful alternative because it
could keep you warm in bed and also catch mice.

nocturnal trip down the corridor in January could result in frostbite.

Essential items for country bedrooms
Capacious clothes storage for all the woollies.
Mothballs.
Full stereo sound and TV.
Warm carpet.
Well-stocked bookcase.
Firm, orthopaedic bed – to restore back strained from all the extra work.
Pleasant, airy pictures of uncontroversial subjects.
Four-poster bed with draught-proof curtains.

Borderline
Magazine rack with glossy country mags.
Dressing table with triple mirror.
Electric trouser press.
Overhead mirror above bed.

Unspeakable
Quasi-erotic pictures, especially modern reproductions of Leda and the Swan or naked men standing on seashores in sunsets.
Anything to do with exercise and fitness.
Automatic teamaker.
Dressing gowns or towels marked 'His' and 'Hers'.
Shag pile.
Anything made of plastic or chromium.

Drawing Room

In the country they are not lounges – those belong in hotels and on ocean liners. Sometimes they are sitting rooms; they may be morning rooms; but mostly they are drawing rooms. How they are 'done out' is important, because they will be seen not perhaps by casual callers but by guests and friends whom you will want to impress.

Country drawing rooms are, nevertheless, usually rather dull and functional. There is often a decent piece or two of furniture – that Regency table groaning under heaped copies of *Field* perhaps, and those pretty Hepplewhite chairs, but these will be lost among a crowd of mainstream furniture and decor which plays safe with comfortable colour combinations – often shades of green – and a style which lacks distinction. When you do come across a room which belongs to an individualist, it can be like a breath of fresh air blowing into a fusty interior.

Colours in established country homes are unspeakably dull. Nobody ever dares to break with convention. A sage-green undertone runs throughout the shires, seldom harmonising with anything other than rustic autumn tints or a series of beiges. Where are the bright oranges, the combinations of sky blue and ginger or navy blue and cerise? Who has gone in for murals or exotic wall hangings or strange cloth wall covering? Very few. Instead, Laura Ashley patterns live on, replaced here and there by William Morris revivals. For the haters of too much patterning, man-made velvet reigns. The glitzy furniture coverings of the nineties are merely cribs of the thirties and novel furniture designs can be found only in the homes of avant-garde types, who are regarded with the deepest suspicion by everyone else in the country.

Worse by far than the avant-garde are the villainous types who have their hi-fi equipment on display but their drinks hidden either in a cupboard or in some appalling kind of cocktail cabinet. There was a time when one could buy false globes or grand pianos which, at the touch of a button, unfolded to reveal a bar stocked with wines, spirits and matching sets of glasses, often crystal or with little gold rings and transfers on them. Such apparatus is the work of Satan and to be shunned. A plain table or trolley burdened with an assortment of bottles, all gathering dust and several with less than an inch in the bottom, is much more the thing.

Though it may be perfectly acceptable to have an unsightly spread of bottles on view, audio systems must never be seen. These should be crammed into the most unlikely receptacles, so that to operate them the owner has to be a contortionist.

Loudspeakers have to be hidden too, even though this renders them barely audible.

Essential items for country drawing rooms

Good oil paintings, preferably nineteenth-century landscapes.
Open fire, preferably log. Inglenooks are fine but must NEVER be decorated with horse brasses.
At least three pieces of antique furniture – inherited antiques are really *the* thing.
Musical instrument, preferably piano or harpsichord.
Really comfortable furniture – but tatty.
Trolley or table with drinks on it.
Hidden source of hi-fi.
Well-stocked bookshelves – real books.
Home-made sloe gin.

Borderline

Flowering plants in pots.
Drinks cupboard.
Nests of tables.
Coffee-table books.
Country Life and *Horse and Hind* on display while *Weekend Sport* and *News of the World* are hidden away.
Flowers in vases.
Hunting prints.
Stuffed animals.

Unspeakable

Reproductions of Old Masters.
Naked televisions or radios.
Cocktail cabinets.
Fake tigerskin rugs.
Fancy flower arrangements, especially with dried material.
False bookbacks, installed by the yard.

Dining Room

Our dining room is used only on Christmas Day and for dinner parties. Being on a different floor from the other reception rooms makes it even less accessible than most dining rooms, but even in houses where the room abuts the kitchen, dining is seldom done there. In the days of butlers, cooks and serving maids, dining rooms were often placed a medium-length walk away from the kitchens to provide the staff with extra exercise and to protect the diners from the smells and noise of the kitchen. These days, dining rooms are a pain in the neck. They occupy important parts of the house and yet are seldom put to use because most people dine in their kitchens or have some sort of arrangement whereby they eat within hailing distance of the stove and sink.

When it is not Christmas Day and there are no dinner parties planned, our dining-room table is heaped with ironing, clothes awaiting replacement buttons, odd books, parcels of shopping, unwanted junk mail and photographic equipment. Thus, whenever a party is decided upon, the first and most major task of preparation is to clear up the mess. I sometimes wonder what would happen if we gave up entertaining. Would the table disappear under an atomic pile of things 'just popped there for the time being'?

As far as feeding guests is concerned, isn't it time we had a change in etiquette so that it became perfectly proper to feed everyone in the kitchen? We could serve out 'ot dinners straight from saucepan to plate and anyone who wanted second helpings could reach the cooker from where they sat. When the eating was over, everyone could help stack the dishwasher and then repair to the drawing room to get plastered on home-made sloe gin.

Traditionally, dining-room decor is red. This is supposed to stimulate the appetite, but it also makes the room feel small, dark and hot. Dining-room chairs, especially for tall people, are always extremely uncomfortable and dig themselves into the small of the back. There's a branch of Sod's law which says the longer the guest's legs are, the more likely he is to find himself seated up against a table leg. As the evening wears on, the pain dulls into a nagging ache, somewhere around the kidneys, and you begin to wonder how much longer you will be able to bear it. If drawing-room seats are in short supply, one often has to stay at the dining-room table for about four hours – from starter to coffee. So, when planning the decor and furnishing of your dining room, you might bear this in mind. Modern chairs, by the way, are just as uncomfortable as old ones.

There is no need to categorise essentials and unspeakables in dining rooms because really all that is needed are table, chairs and sideboard stocked with silver (real) and porcelain (not pot).

Decorative Terms

You may find that the prospect of making mistakes with your decor scares you into appointing an interiors expert. There will be a huge fee and you may not like the result anyway, but it will save you the headache of worrying about whether the colour schemes, styles and furniture you use are in good or bad taste. The experts will probably try to baffle you with difficult words, so here are a few in frequent use set out with their meanings.

Acrylic Bitter tasting. Water from an acrylic bath is less heavy but more bitter than water from a cast-iron bath.

Aga A type of heavy cast-iron stove. The word is actually an acronym from the words 'Ah, Gone Again', because of their habit of going out.

Anaglypta Perfectly proportioned film-star of the 1930s who is frequently depicted in embossed wallpaper designs.

Antimacassar Person or persons who are set against the establishment (cf. Antimacasablanca – a hatred of Bogart films – and Antimacasapupo – a hatred of porcelain fruit).

Bath chair A bath shaped like a chair so the bather can sit with water up to his neck; less frequently, a chair shaped like a bath, but without the taps.

Bituminous Unpleasant, biting, sarcastic.

Chaise longue A horse-drawn carriage with six wheels in tandem (cf. Gingham).

Char-a-banc A wooden settle put out in ancient times by banks who had queues at their cashpoints.

Commode A man who trades in large, bulky materials like wheat, potatoes, ores or coffee futures.

Compendium A set of flats or houses bought and run by a group of people.

Couch Someone who trains sportsmen or teams.

Dado Queen of Carthage who loved Aeneas; subject of many operas and plays.

Davenport A kind of bag specially designed for carrying davens. In certain parts of the country, a warming beverage to be consumed at home.

Diffuser The standard lamp that blows the fuses when you trip over the flex.

Efflorescence Fizziness caused by water hitting the health salts (in the wall).

Flush hob Part of the lavatory where the handle disappears into the cistern housing.

Frieze Technique for setting rows of plaster shapes by blowing air at minus 2° C over them.

Gingham An eighteenth-century horse-drawn vehicle with two wheels and isinglass curtains for changes in weather (cf. *Chaise longue*).

Grouting A form of hunting where the quarry – usually hares or rabbits – is tracked down by packs of small terriers.

Loggia Place to store firewood.

Mural Name of a female painter so famous she has become synonymous with frescoes and wall paintings.

Pelmet Reinforced headdress.

Polyurethane Thick resin painted round lavatories to prevent leakage problems.

Putty Cloth wound round the lower leg.

Receding colours Colours which fade, disappearing completely within a year of being applied. They cost more than ordinary colours, as you would expect.

Scrim A short, high-pitched cry, usually uttered on first sight of your decorator's invoice.

Settee *see* Sofa.

Silent gliss A form of mould which develops behind curtains and spreads wherever there is anything covering the wall.

Shag pile Deep, luxurious carpet designed for sleeping on and, er, things like that.

Sofa *see* Settee.

Swag Stolen booty, especially curtain material.

Sybaritic Describing a sufferer of sybariasis, a disease caused by excesses of luxury.

Syphonic suite A series of pieces of music played by a syphony orchestra.

Tallboy A gigolo of five foot eleven or more.

Vinyl Associated with grapes.

Welsh dresser A cumbersome piece of furniture, compulsory in certain country kitchens, too big to get in (or out of) the house. Nothing to do with Welsh dressing.

The road to good decor, in the country, is to be unpretentious. Synthetic coachlamps, fake outdoor shutters and a garden pond floodlit in red and blue light are not really the thing. Even putting a small sign up stating the name of your house is regarded as being slightly pushy, which is a shame, because it means that nobody knows where anyone else lives. Artificial diagonal leaded lights in the windows are unspeakable, but the worst possible mistake is to colour-wash your exterior in a bright shade of blue, green or pink. This would mark you down as a rank outsider.

Just to make sure you are by now well acquainted with the subject, here are some exercises.

1 Which of the following would be unspeakable in a tasteful country home?
(a) Small indoor fountain which lights up and is decorated with simulated flowers, **(b)** lifesize bust of Nigel Lawson converted to a standard lamp, **(c)** labrador, **(d)** glass-fronted gun cupboard in drawing room.

2 How would you set about plucking and drawing five brace of pheasant, a teal and four brace of partridge without making a mess in the kitchen?

Synthetic coachlamps, fake outdoor shutters and a
garden pond floodlit in red and blue light are not
really the thing.

3 Which colours are ideal in the following rooms of a country house?
(a) Bedroom, **(b)** bathroom, **(c)** drawing room, **(d)** lavatory, **(e)** dining room, **(f)** garage.

4 What is the difference between a patio and a terrace?
(a) Fifty years, **(b)** £40,000 per annum, **(c)** your family background.

Answers

1 'Tasteful' is not what matters; we're after comfort.

2 Send them to the village butcher with a bottle of scotch and a dinner invitation.

3 Sage green.

4 Could be any of these.

Chapter 7

Sympathetic Conversions

Except ye be converted . . . ye shall not enter into the Kingdom of Heaven.

(Matthew 18:3)

With such an exodus into the country these days, it's hardly surprising that so few decent houses are available and that so many people are desperately seeking the perfect rural des. res. One result of all this pressure on the market has been a phenomenal increase in the number of conversions.

For some inexplicable reason, considerable kudos can be had from living in a house that has been converted from something else. The more outlandish the original use of the building, the bigger the cachet – the bigger the cash outlay too. Barns, granaries, dairies and stable blocks are pretty usual, but police stations, Wesleyan chapels and old village schools carry more distinction. For the truly offbeat, conversion opportunities are rarer, but there are people living in converted signal boxes, railway stations, telephone exchanges and even fire stations. If you want to end up in a really outlandish home, you'll have to keep your ear to the ground and pounce as soon as there is the merest suspicion of something convertible coming up for sale.

Whatever happens, you should be fully aware of the basic rules of conversion. These could make profound changes to your happiness and run as follows:

1 All conversions cost a great deal more than you ever thought

possible. If you decide to do the work yourself, time and again the hidden costs will take you by surprise. Walls which you thought sound will prove to have shifted several degrees from the vertical and others, once you have decided to knock them down, will prove to be triple reinforced with concrete and metal concealed down their centres. If you think I'm exaggerating, just remember that the barn was previously used as a grain store and imagine what pressure a 500 tonne heap of wheat can exert on a structural wall. If it hasn't moved, it's reinforced; if it isn't reinforced, it will have moved.

When builders do the work, you will find that major repairs which they overlooked during the conversion job cause structural failure at the worst possible moment, after you've moved in, and not only do you have to rebuild part of the house, you also have to rip out bathrooms and kitchen to do it.

2 No conversion ever makes a truly habitable house. However skilfully your farm building has been adapted for modern use, you will always be living a compromise. At best, it will feel like living in a barn; at worst – well, you could always hope for a fire and a total rebuild.

3 Every conversion job is a building experiment. If you have had five or six stabs at converting your barn, the chances of getting everything right, finally, are reasonable. But how many cardinal errors can you afford? Most can manage only one, so all the years you spend living in your conversion will be frustrated by knowing exactly how you would rebuild it if only you had realised at the time what a beam at head height above the kitchen door meant in terms of injured skulls and if only the hole under the 400-year-old oak door, where the icy air creeps in, had been repaired before the new floor was installed above it.

4 Conversions are usually ugly. A barn full of cattle with a haystack outside and an old haywain, or even a Morris Minor, parked near it looks picturesque, especially if there's a scattering of mud-caked peasants nearby, wallowing about in abject poverty – as per eighteenth-century oil paintings. A barn with windows cut into its walls and frilly curtains looks a bit silly. A 1930s phone box with frilly curtains, window boxes and 'Ringham Lodge' or 'Bell Cottage' printed on the door looks even sillier.

5 Conversions are hard to sell. Prospective buyers are quick to see the pitfalls and can be very shy about committing themselves.

6 Conversions seldom have good gardens. More often than not, the farmer who sells off a building wants to maximise his return without losing any land, so frequently he sells the barn plus a tiny apron of concrete for car parking. You may not mind, as long as there are good views over open countryside, but when it's too late you find out about his plans to erect a 5,000-square-foot grain store – for which he doesn't need planning permission – within a few yards of your front door.

Even if the site gives the illusion of a garden, the chances are the builders have merely scattered a thin layer of topsoil about and laid a token patio. Dig into the ground and you'll jar your elbow when the spade meets solid hardcore two inches down.

If you are still determined to go for a conversion in spite of having heard all these negative noises, you must have great courage. Very commendable, but you're in for a bumpy ride. Prepare for the worst!

Converting Yourself

Like being a born-again Christian, you must have unshakable faith. You will need to decide, first, whether to do your own converting or whether to rely on someone else's taste and handiwork – remembering that other people's handiwork may not be very handy.

Having decided to do your own conversion, your next task is to decide what type of house you want. How much can you afford? However cheap the barn or shed may look when you select it, the price tag on the finished article is what *really* matters. There is a fairly simple formula for working this out. First, decide on the number of bedrooms you want. Multiply that figure by £50,000, add to that the cost of the original building and then add the legal costs. (These will be much higher than with ordinary house purchases because there will be unbelievable complications like Ancient Lights, rights of the local hunt to pass through the barn in October, the vendor retaining licences to abstract water from a well under the kitchen floor and so on.) To that total, add 20 per cent of the figure. Got that? Good. Well, for a greenfield site, that is a site where there are no buildings, services or even a road, the figure you now have would be roughly accurate. However, for a conversion, the essential services, foundations and many of the walls are already there, so you must do one more simple calculation. Divide the total by 0.5.

Thus:

	£
Site plus barn	65,000
Legal costs	6,000
Bedrooms (4)	200,000
Total	271,000
Plus 20 per cent	54,200
Grand total	325,200
Therefore cost of finished conversion	650,400

So, by an extraordinary coincidence, the house you end up with costs ten times the price of the original barn. Of course, this would be in favourable circumstances. Costs are frequently higher.

If you've been sensible enough to buy your own copy of this extremely helpful book, I am assuming that finding the odd three-quarters of a million will not pose any problem at all. If I'm not right, perhaps you ought to abandon the idea of doing a conversion. Well, have you made up your mind? Good, let's get on, then.

The next job is to decide what to convert. The smallest conversion ever was of a police phone box, completed on 23 November 1963. Normally, this would hardly have been worthwhile, but the person who designed it managed to make it more roomy on the inside than the outside dimensions allowed. The result was thirty years of adventurous living, apparently in a sand quarry populated by motorised dustbins. I'm afraid I can't remember who it was. Too Ancient; Recently Died, I Suspect.

Most converted buildings look the other way round – huge on the outside but turning out to be poky and cramped within.

Barns make the roomiest buildings, but so many of them are long and thin. This means that every room has at least two outside walls – cold – and that it is impossible to go into one room without passing through another. The alternative is a narrow passage down one side. Stables can make grand houses and often carry some accommodation already. This can help if you are actually doing the physical work of the conversion yourself, because at least you'll have somewhere to sleep while you work. Just remember, though, that stable accommodation was luxurious for horses in bygone days, but that grooms were expected to survive in rat-infested lofts with nothing but a rusty harness to serve as a pillow, the only luxury supplied by their employers being a pickaxe to break the ice on the horse trough in which they were allowed to wash every second Thursday, after the horses had drunk their fill.

With the decline of almost every church in Britain, ecclesiastical buildings have become quite popular for conversion lately – not the kind St Paul had in mind, evidently. They carry perplexing problems, the chief of which is that they usually have long, narrow windows, which makes it awkward to know just where to position the floor which is to provide an upstairs. If the windows are stained glass, you have little choice but to slice the religious scenes in half, so that people in the drawing room can admire the feet of the Apostles, who decorate the master bedroom from the waist up.

A friend of mine has recently negotiated to buy a railway signal box. It is actually a listed building and so his conversion will have to be very sympathetic. The place is beautifully lit – windows all round – but the external stairs will prove a bit draughty in winter and I don't suppose he'll have room upstairs for an *en-suite* loo. As for sleeping arrangements, no doubt he'll have to sling a couple of hammocks from the signal levers. Apparently, his alarm clock will be a trembler bell, stimulated by the 6.38 on the 'up' line when it comes through every morning, bang on time, at 7.20 – or thereabouts.

Oast houses are romantic because they go with everyone's image of rural Kent, the Garden of England. Nowadays, when living in Kent means life in the fast lane, the idea of tranquil hop gardens, apple orchards and trout-rich chalk streams is as absurd as hoping to find Eliza Doolittle in Floral Street. However, though they no longer dry hops, those lovely rounded buildings of mellow brickwork, topped with dunce's hat roofs, are nearly all being lived in by prosperous professionals. They are quite unsuitable for serious consideration, of course, because they are such an awkward shape. Downstairs, there is a huge, windowless void in the centre – wonderful for photographers who want darkroom facilities or for vampires who want coffin space, but hardly conducive to gracious living and rotten for day-time entertaining. Upstairs, if you try to develop into the roof space, the bedrooms get smaller and smaller with each floor. The occupant of the top floor has to sleep to attention, but he does have the advantage of a winch outside to lower himself to the ground or to hoist up breakfast, Sunday papers, mistress or whatever. Oast houses are often built right on the roadside, which was fine when the road was a rustic lane but is not so good now it's the M2.

Windmills are romantic but impossible. First of all, you need to have all your furniture made with special rounded backs, so that it all fits to the walls. Eventually, the occupants develop rounded backs too. The other point about windmills is that all the rooms are on top of one another, so you spend the whole time sprinting up and down stairs.

Old wharves are nearly as bad, being tall and thin and having misleading doors which open to thin air on every floor as well as the ground. These were for lowering heavy loads down on to ships but can be extraordinarily useful for pain-in-the-arse guests.

'My dear, how *do* you manage with all these stairs?'

'Oh, it keeps us pretty fit.'

'But it's so *hopelessly* impractical.'

'Oh, we love it. Such super views down the river.'

'Mm. Wouldn't suit Derek and me. By the way, where's your loo?'

'Two flights up. Red door facing you at the top of the stairs.'

'Right. Send a search party if I don't show in ten mins, what? Ha ha. Oh, two flights? Really, I don't know how you cope.'

Goes upstairs. Rattling door handle.

'A A A A A A a a a a . . . ' SPLASH!!!!!!!

'Oh, did I say red door? Sorry, I meant blue.'

Having found the conversion opportunity of your dreams, the next obstacle to overcome is the vendor. Say you've picked on a delicious roadside barn at the top end of a traditional farmyard. The mellow walls are built with honey-coloured limestone and the roof is clad with lichened slates. Your mind's eye dismisses the cracks in the stonework and the ominous bulge in the west wall, conjuring up instead fragrant honeysuckle and old moss roses tumbling round the door and a contented cat sleeping on the windowsill. A perfect Thomas Hardy image. Conveniently, you forget that most of Hardy's characters come horrendously unstuck! The barn is on the market, that's all you know. You think the vendor's estate agent is being cagey about the price and no one seems to know how much land goes with it, so you decide to cut the formalities and approach the vendor direct.

'Could you tell me a little more about these boundaries?' you say, as an opening gambit. He seems helpful and polite, but you don't know what's going on beneath that inscrutable exterior.

'Well, the agent has the details, but I'll do what I can.'

'Fine, well, er, does the proposed boundary run here?'

'Not sure really. I thought they were going to knock in a white post or something. Well, hereabouts, I suppose.'

'Could you be a little more precise?'

'Ah, well, I'm sure it is just here. Well, about here. More or less.'

'What about the main access. Would you still be using it?'

'Oh yes, but no problem there. We could share the cost of maintenance, I should think.'

'And the walls – boundary walls, I mean?'

'You'd be better to leave them intact, for your own privacy really.'

'What about where the gaps are? Would we have to build walls there?'

'I don't think so. Well, perhaps some sort of dividing fence. You know, just a token divider.'

'What about price?'

'Oh, I'm afraid you'd have to ask my agent about that.'

'But have you any idea at all?'

'I'd rather you spoke to my agent.'

'I heard you'd refused an offer of fifty thou.'

'Did you? Well, my, my!' A pause, then, 'I say, look, can I interest you in tickets for our parish Cheese and Wine? It's next week. You could meet all the locals.'

Eventually you buy. For £70,000. When the contract has been drawn up, you find out that 'shared' maintenance of the road means that you are responsible to 80 per cent of the costs, even though he will be using it for all his heavy farm equipment. All existing boundary walls, you read, must now be maintained by you and kept in perfect condition – although they look as though they might fall down if you lean on them at present – and where a new boundary exists, you are to build external walls to eight feet in old stone to match the 'general good quality' of the stone buildings. But by now you have fallen in love with the old place and regard it as nearly yours. You sign the contract and all that remains between today and moving in are months of building works.

Next you must suffer the slings and arrows of outrageous bureaucracy. Because you are unlucky enough to have bought your barn in a conservation area, life will be a continuum of frustration. The barn probably carried only outline planning permission, so your next task is to get the details buttoned up. This will turn out to be rather more than the mere formality you anticipated. For a start, the locals will be lying in wait. They'll have raised all kinds of objections and will have secured Tree Preservation Orders on every scrap of vegetation, including the birch tree growing out of the stonework on the north elevation. The planning office will have an architectural consultant who has the final say on what exact form your conversion should take. She (it could just as easily be a he) will be keen to expose her superior knowledge and good taste. Your own plans, however brilliant you may think they are, will come in for some pretty drastic alterations. These will not be for the best. In fact, by the time she has shown you what the planning office would find acceptable, you will wonder whether to abandon the entire project and move back to town.

Don't think that once your completed plans are approved, you will be left alone. Your friendly expert from the planning office will keep popping in the whole way through the building operation to advise on everything from foundation materials to the type

Your own plans will come in for some pretty drastic
alteration.

of paint on the inside walls of the cupboard under the stairs. Architectural consultants' tastes vary enormously and each one has his or her own special little quirks – a fixation on louvred shutters, let's say, or an abhorrence of down pipes. When dealing with them, you must never forget that:

1 They have tremendous power and could scupper all your plans at any stage.

2 You are an ignorant Philistine and cannot possibly know what is a tasteful conversion and what is an unsightly botch-up. Therefore all your opinions must be subordinate to those of the expert.

3 In principle, they are dead against all conversions and most forms of development anyway, so you are on a losing wicket from the start.

A friend of mine once bought a derelict watermill miles from anywhere. The architectural expert imposed on him by the planning office hadn't a positive thought in his head. This was made clear right from the first meeting.

'I don't understand why you want to convert this mill in the first place, Mr Spokeshave. Why not leave it as it is?'

'But it's derelict. Falling down.'

'I mean, leave it as a watermill.'

'We want to live in it.'

'I find this craze for converting things hard to understand.'

'But it's such a beautiful spot, tucked away here deep in the valley by this little stream. It's a wonderful place to live.'

'For a watermill, perhaps.'

'Well, we're planning to keep as much of the mill as possible intact. I plan to restore the wheel and we shall keep the moving parts of the mill inside too.'

'Why?'

'Historical interest. The wheel itself is unique. We'll have to get a proper blacksmith to recast some of the spokes, but I've never seen a wheel this age in such good condition. It's restorable. A wonderful example of pre-Victorian industry.'

'I trust you won't be grinding or milling anything.'

'Why not?'

'You don't have planning consent to do that. It would constitute a change of use and, since this is a conservation area, you'd stand no chance of getting approval.'

'I thought you wanted it to stay as a watermill.'

'Oh certainly, but not working.'

'How then?'

'Just left alone, unaltered.'

'Collapsed, you mean?'

'I think you should be a little more cooperative, Mr Spokeshave. After all, nothing has been approved yet.'

Getting back to your barn, having sorted everything out with the planners and architects, you are ready to start building. From day one, the hidden snags will appear. Once I managed to borrow a page or two from a near neighbour's diary. He bought a barn very similar to yours last year. He hopes he'll be moving in before next Christmas but . . .

13 August
Progress at last! Building starts tomorrow. The JCB is due to arrive at seven-thirty. Foundation trenches for extension and drains will take less than a day to dig. JCB man came in his car to have a look. Charming man. Says it'll be a doddle.

14 August
JCB man started. Unearthed a well sixty feet deep at eight am. Said he wouldn't drive no more until he knew what else there was under the yard. Went home. Rather unpleasant about it, I thought. Not charming at all.

15 August
No work done. Waiting for buildings expert to advise.

16 August
Expert unable to come. Pressure of work, he said.

17 August
Expert twisted ankle. Off work.

18 August
Still no expert. Hay fever.

19 August

Rang planning office. Expert is back at work but had to go to Brussels.

20 August

Expert due to come but plane held up. Spent night at airport (the expert, not me – though sorely tempted).

21 August

No work done for seven days now, but JCB standing by so having to pay full hire charge, but daren't let it go because of three-week waiting period to rehire. Expert has disappeared. His office knows his flight took off but nothing more.

22 August

Expert has been! Well is eighty feet deep, not sixty, and must be filled and made safe. He says there cannot possibly be any other wells in same yard.

23 August

JCB man has dug huge hole to get soil to fill the well. He says it's what that there Buildings Regulation man ordered him to do. Got quite offensive when I asked what he would use to fill in the hole he had made.

24 August

JCB back wheel cracked the cover of a second well. This one only thirty feet deep. JCB man has given his notice. Says he's going to work for Motorway Maintenance, because it's safer.

10 September

At last, both wells have been made safe and the hole filled up again, this time with spoil from the motorway construction site. We're ready to start digging the drains.

11 September

New JCB man, Bert, has arrived. Much brighter than the last one. Actually talks rather than grunts. Says it will be less than half a day to complete such a little job but he has to finish a little plastering he was doing for a mate, 'on the side, like', and will be back tomorrow. Odd, but JCB firm rang to say a driver called Bert was due to come but was away sick at the moment. Nothing serious, they assured me, and he'd be with me in a day or two.

15 September
Bert, the JCB man, says he's finished the plastering for his mate and will do our job tomorrow. Said to order the concrete. I've fixed a lorry load for four tomorrow afternoon.

16 September
Bert (JCB) arrived at 2.27 pm. Half an hour later, the trench for the foundations was half dug when he found the underground petrol tank. Said a single spark could cause a vast explosion. Said I'd no business putting him at risk like that. Should have told them about it. I said I'd no idea the tank was there. He said I should have had the place surveyed properly. I said I had and nothing had been said about any petrol pump or tank. He said I was a bloody amateur and ought to have more bloody sense than to go causing bloody explosions. Said all that with a fag hanging out of his mouth, but when I pointed that out he said I was bleedin' ignorant. Then the concrete arrived. They dumped nearly half the load into the wrong trench – the one dug for the drains – before I noticed they were there at all. It will all have to be dug out again. By the time I'd stopped them shooting any more of the concrete into the trench, Bert was walking down the track to his car. I begged him not to desert me. Really grovelled. He said he'd come back when the fire brigade have tested the fuel tank for safety.

17 September
Rang the fire brigade. I'd tried yesterday but they said they only came to cases like that during office hours. Said they'd need three weeks' notice.

1 October
The fire brigade have tested the tank. It was made safe seventeen years ago, according to their records. The officer said if only I'd told them where the tank was in the first place, they could have

told me that from their records and saved themselves a time-wasting visit. If he didn't know where the tank was, I asked him, how did he know where to come? That stumped him, but he developed a sinister glint in his eye and said he'd be back to measure the distance between our barn and the farmer's walls. Something about a fire hazard and blocking further building. Bert comes back to finish trenching next week.

8 October
At last, the foundation work is finished and the drain pipes are in! I can't believe it. We start on the real building tomorrow. Gave Bert a bottle of whisky. He said he was more of a rum and pep man hisself but thanks anyway.

10 October
Clive, the brickie, has arrived. Bert tells me he's the fastest mortar-slapper going. His hands move so fast you can't see 'em. Quite true. I've never seen anything quite like it, but he seems to lay bricks only for about half an hour at a stretch and then has to drink a thermos of tea and have a nap to recover his strength.

11 October
Disastrous news. The main wall of the barn is unsound. Digging the foundations for the extensions has caused movement. The whole wall must be demolished and rebuilt.

Are you getting the idea of how it goes now? Still want to convert?

Ghosts, Ghoulies and Goolies

Ghosts are by no means special to conversions but this seems as good a place as any to explain how to deal with them. Every country home built before 1950 has one. When a house is on the market, the owner often has a difficult time deciding whether to admit that it is haunted or whether to keep mum about it. There is a certain distinction about having your own domestic ghost,

If a large stone ball falls off the gateway and rolls
uphill over your toes, the house has a poltergeist.

indeed, it can be a good selling point, but handled tactlessly, it could also scare off nervous buyers. That is why, if ghosts are talked about at all, they are always benign ones, working up a sympathy vote rather than unbridled terror. You'll be told of a 'grey lady' or a 'white lady' or a ragged child with pallid features carrying a posy. When viewing houses, you never hear about skeletons which do rugby tackles from behind wardrobes, or ghoulish figures which materialise at twelve minutes past two in the morning of 15 February every year and threaten to claw out the homeowner's eyes.

Vendors also keep pretty quiet about poltergeists, which are almost wholly sinister. If, when you are viewing a property, a turret falls off the west wing, missing you by inches but crushing the owner's Pekinese, the most likely explanation is structural unsoundness – unless the TV aerial man is avenging a bitten ankle. If, on the other hand, a large stone ball falls off the gateway and rolls *uphill* over your toes, the house has a poltergeist and the haunting spirit is making it pretty clear that it doesn't like the cut of your jib. I should look for another house.

With conversions, what upsets the ghosts is that you are making big changes to their environment. This will make them restless and they are sure to haunt you unless you get a spiritual whitewash job done by the local vicar. In our friend's watermill, the problem was centred round the mill wheel. When his restored model was connected to the shaft and began turning, the most spine-chilling groaning started and continued for ages, scaring everybody to death and making them run howling out of the house and up the lane. It wasn't until they plucked up the courage to go back and oil the ancient bearings that, like magic, the groaning stopped.

When you convert your barn, apprentices drowned in wells, maidens ravished in haylofts and farmers who fell on their pitch-forks will tend to rise up in a body and rattle your resolve – but they won't disturb your nights half as much as the thoughts of how high interest rates might go and what your mortgage will cost per month if the Chancellor of the Exchequer slaps on yet another ½ per cent. Conversions are not for the weak-willed.

Ready Converted

If all these tales of woe are putting you off the idea of doing your own conversion, you could still consider buying something that has already been turned into a home. This has the advantage of allowing you to move in quickly, without going through any of the agony of doing your own building. However, there are still plenty of pitfalls set out to entrap the unwary. How good, for example, is the quality of the workmanship? Were the best possible materials used? Was everything installed correctly? What comeback have you if anything goes wrong?

Take a typical situation. Jeremy and Samantha Redbrace, the Young Perspirer couple, have been living in their converted slaughterhouse on the banks of the River Mudde for the last two years. It's a lovely June Sunday morning. Jeremy is putting the patio loungers out by the swimming pool while Samantha makes the bed. Suddenly he hears a shriek.

'Jer! Halp!!!' He looks up at the bedroom to see Samantha hanging out of the frame, holding the window in her hand.

'What's the matter, Bunnypops?'

'Halp! The window!'

'What's the matter with the window?'

'I'm holding it, you cretin!'

'I can see that, Pudding, but what's wrong?'

'The sodding thing's come off. Look.' And, before Jeremy can say Financial Times Ordinary Share Index, the silly cow has let go and the entire simulated Georgian casement has crashed to the ground, annihilating the drinks trolley and cell phone in one blow. They have a rot problem. Next day, when Jeremy's safely back in the City, mismanaging his investors' funds and trying to kick his Perrier habit, Samantha has the builder in again – that nice little man, Percy, by whom everyone swears and who charges so little as long as you pay cash.

'More coffee?' she says, reaching for the complicated piece of lab equipment that has been making obscenely biological noises in the corner of the kitchen. 'I hope you like this. It's pure wild Ethiopian with just a bean or two of burnt Colombian. Ya?'

'Do what?'

'Coffee.'

'Oh yeah. Look, do you think we could have a look at this 'ere winder?'

'Oh sure. Come this way.'

They go upstairs, Percy trying not to let his eyes widen too much at the excess of frilly underwear and nighties and things there are lying about the bedroom. He looks at the hole where the window was. Sharp intake of breath. He rolls a fag and cups it in his hand, the glowing end hidden, takes an amazingly deep drag, exhales, repeats the process, delicately nudges the ash from the cigarette into the little Sèvres bonbon dish she uses for her rings overnight and purses his lips.

'Cor,' he says.

'I *know*.' She agrees.

'Winder's gorn,' he says.

'That's rather what we thought.'

He pokes about among the broken frame, digging here and there with his screwdriver.

'Rotten timber.'

'I know. I suppose it happens with old timber. The original frames are Victorian.'

'Old? Nar, the old stuff's OK. It's these new winders what've rotted. Look.' He prods, lifting a flake of paint. 'Not properly primed or painted. Who did this job? Ought to be shot.'

'Skregthorpe Construction.'

'Oh well. Say ner more!'

'But they've a very good reputation.'

'Yeah? Well, there's reputations 'n' reputations. Let's have a look at the other winders.' They go to the next bedroom. He prods again. 'Thought so. Look. This one's as bad.' He opens it, leans out backwards and looks up. 'Ah!' he says, voice sounding funny from the outside. 'There's yer problem. Gutters put up wrong.'

'Is that serious?'

'Depends 'ow long you want yer 'ouse to stay up.' A second roll-your-own fag. This time the ash goes into Samantha's Meissen candlestick. 'If yer winder's rotted that fast, I'd say most of the damage is already done.'

'Oh dear! Can you put it right?'

A mammoth intake of breath, another drag on the cigarette, inhaled so deeply no smoke comes out when he exhales. At this point Samantha makes a really major boob. She says, 'Look. I don't mind what it costs, as long as you can put it right.'

He manages, just, to resist exclaiming in triumph. Instead, he takes another drag and mutters: ''ave ter see what we can do, won't we. Start a week as Wednesday.'

Now he's got his meal ticket, the tension subsides. He pinches the end out of his fag, returning the unsmoked centimetre to his baccy tin. She realises she has fallen into the trap.

'Have you *any* idea of what it might cost?'

'Couldn't say, lady. Not till we've got all the rotted wood chopped out.'

'How long will that take?'

'Hard to say. Have to chop it all out first before we can put noo winders in.'

The harsh reality takes a while to dawn on Samantha. Finally, the penny drops.

'But, you mean we'll have no windows?'

'Only for a foo weeks. We c'n put plastic sheetin' on.'

'But we won't be secure.'

'Yeeees! Thick poly'll keep the weather art!'

'I'm not thinking about that. What about burglars?'

'Ah.'

That's a poser. Percy lights another fag.

When you go househunting for that ideal conversion, there are certain phrases in the estate agents' blurb which should sound serious warning bells. These will be set out as selling points but it's essential that you understand the underlying meaning.

With many original features means that there are bits which the builders weren't quite sure about. In old flour mills, for example, they would leave old shafts, still bristling with pulleys and cogs, because there is nothing else to hold the walls in. The only problem is that the same shaft runs aross the master bedroom ceiling at head height, making it look like a half-built factory. (Well, let's face it, that's exactly what it is – a half-unbuilt factory.) This is fine if you're into Dada but most people prefer a bedroomious decor. Furthermore, the risk of braining yourself on such original features is high.

Few original features are really very original. The golden syrup tin, wedged into the hole in the staircase with Polyfilla could hardly be called original, neither could the asbestos roof over the scullery, nor the strange-looking metal cowl over the inglenook – the one that has the words 'Massey Ferguson' stencilled on the inside.

Sympathetically converted means that they have hardly touched the main structure at all and have not therefore got to grips with the main structural faults. These will become apparent a few months after you've moved in. If, when you paper over a crack in the plaster, it reappears within six weeks, your walls are on the move. Start sleeping in a crash helmet. When you hammer a nail in to hang a picture, if a whole building stone behind the plasterboard pushes out of place, so that the nail sinks in to its head in one tap, call in a structural engineer.

In conservation village means you can't do anything with it unless you have full planning permission, and getting that is about as likely as finding 200 gold sovereigns stashed away in that golden syrup tin we were talking about.

Large, studio room refers to the bulk of the upper-floor area, which the architect, for several reasons, was unable to incorporate into bedrooms or put to any other use for that matter. Hardly surprising, since it has no windows and its ceiling height is four foot eleven.

Superb converted watermill on River Ooze in an area of outstanding natural beauty means a damp house straddling a stream with flooding in winter and invasions of trippers all summer. Park a boat or a caravan in your drive for more than ten minutes and you'll have Greenpeace and the CPRE threatening you for damaging the environment. Spot a hawfinch in your garden and 4,000 twitchers will be trampling your veg garden into a mouldering bog within the day. The legs of their heavy-duty telescope tripods will play havoc with the cucumber frames and the hawfinches will have been scared away, never to return.

Thoughtfully modernised means the builders installed the minimum number of mod cons but gave a great deal of thought to how they should be placed for minimum inconvenience – to themselves.

Thoughtfully modernised to highest standards means the same but the bath taps are plated with fake gold.

An important conversion means the agents don't quite know what else to say about it.

You don't really want to convert anything now, do you? Of course you don't. Why not go for one of those nice Wimpatt homes they're putting up. No ghosts, no worries about rot or anything. Nice sensible neighbours. What? You still like the idea? You *are* a glutton for punishment, aren't you.

Here are a few exercises for you.

1 Think up aptly pretentious names for the following conversions. Examples are included for your guidance, but try to be a little more imaginative if you can.

Ex-abattoir – '*La Viande Rose*'. Ex-police station – 'Old Nick's'. Ex-windmill – 'The Overdraught'. Ex-smithy – 'The Old Forgery'. Ex-pub – 'de Boos Hall'. Ex-watermill – 'The Long Drop'.

2 Which of the following is most suitable for conversion?
(a) A medieval stone barn, (b) a disused railway station, (c) a Victorian granary, (d) a furniture van, (e) a delicensed country pub?

3 When deciding to undertake your own conversion, which professional will you consult first?
(a) A builder, (b) an architect, (c) the planning officer, (d) a structural engineer, (e) the local midwife?

Answers

2 Obviously the furniture van, because (a) you can do what you like to it without planning consent, (b) you can travel in it and therefore avoid having to pay poll tax, and (c) it will be much easier to sell after conversion than any of the others.

3 Your bank manager.

Chapter 8

Household Pests

**Putrefaction is the end
Of all that Nature doth intend**

(Robert Herrick)

Yes, that *is* rather a sinister-looking patch, isn't it. No, not that one – that's where you let the bath overflow. Came right through the ceiling, didn't it? Funny how it ran out through the light fixture. No wonder the fuses all went. No, I mean that other patch, further round, on the new plastering. Sort of furry, isn't it? With a darker rim on the edge. Goodness! It feels damp. Got an odd smell too, hasn't it? Ooh look, there's another one over there, under the windowsill. That one's got little black spots as well as fur. Smells like a mouldy breadbin. Then there's the little one you noticed yesterday, by the door. Are you sure it isn't a bit bigger today? I think it is . . . yes . . . you could cover it with one hand yesterday, couldn't you? Has your hand shrunk, d'you think? No. It's a problem. Another problem. Just when you thought the insulating bill was the last you'd have to pay for a while. Better get the builders in again.

Of course, your biggest mistake was thinking you could make your dream home draught-proof. I'm not suggesting you can't. Most energy economists are bubbling over with jolly ideas about double glazing your leaded lights and lagging your rafters. Trouble is, those same experts all live in nice, cosy, modern houses in Esher. Not for them the mouldering kingpins, crumbling ridge tiles or deathwatch beetles. In theory, plugging all the holes and double glazing the windows of your period pile makes good sense. In practice, if you insulate, all you are doing is mollycoddling the bugs. The choice is straightforward: freeze in winter or be warm while your house decays round you.

All old houses, however tastefully restored, are in a state of decay. Refurbishing merely provides a false sense of security. Under the Wilton, behind the watered-silk wall covering and above all, between ceiling and roof, the pests are at work. That is why so many owners of old houses love Wagner. It's the only music loud enough to drown the sounds of insects munching, timber cracking and rodents boring. Life in an old house means keeping one step ahead of the pests. Sometimes you win, sometimes they do. This chapter is intended not to help you to defeat your pests – they are invincible – but to learn to live in harmony with them. Who knows, you may grow to love them. If you don't, you'll be back to the Smoke ere long, mark my words.

The first and most important skill you must learn is to identify your pest. Every pest that affects your home directly – let's call them primary pests – carries its own set of secondaries. For example, woodworm leads, inevitably, to an invasion of pest-control operators. Bats in your roof will conjure up a veritable squad of conservationists. Children always bring friends home and so on. You must, if you wish to control your pest, strike at the very roots of the primary problem. Here some typical pest problems. Let's have a look at the smallest first.

Microbial Pests and Plants

These are the really nasty ones. You can't usually see them but the results of their presence are horribly visible. Basically they fall into one of about five categories: fungi, bacteria, mosses, weeds and Jehovah's Witnesses.

Fungi are the most dramatic. Those patches we've just been looking at are fungi but, being friendly little souls, they are probably inviting bacteria to set up house with them and, who knows, there might even be an alga or two who decides to share the same patch. Fungi spores are in the air. Even while you read this, you are breathing them in and out of your lungs – well into them, anyway. Oh, don't be alarmed. You've been doing it all your life! My first major encounter with a serious fungus was at my public school. (You can always tell people who went to minor public schools. If the schools had been major, it would have been, 'When I was at Charterhouse,' or, 'Of course, we never did it that way at Winchester.' Only those dragged through one of the lesser establishments, like most cathedral schools or Harrow, will refer just to 'my public school.') Anyway, at my public school, we had lurking about the premises a carpenter who was known as Chippy – we were always very original in our allocation of sobriquets. This Chippy was an odd character and we teenagers were anxious to avoid him because of his tendency to hang around the changing rooms. There were always duckboards to repair in the shower room just when we were getting cleaned up after rugby and we felt decidedly insecure when he was around. One afternoon, having conned my way out of cricket on the pretence of having exams to swat for, I was in my study getting stuck into a Dennis Wheatley when Chippy burst in.

'Follow me, boy,' he commanded, with such conviction and so bright a gleam of zeal in his eye that I obeyed without question.

'Where are we going?' I asked, suddenly aware that the house was completely empty apart from the two of us.

'Cellar!'

'Oh er?' I was beginning to hear alarm bells. Nobody ever went into the cellar except for a quick, illicit cigarette. It was dark, cold and soundproof. 'I'm, er, not sure.' I hung back.

'Come on, boy. I'm going to show you something extraordinary and revolting.'

Now I was getting really scared. He was bigger than I was. His huge hand gripped my arm.

'But . . . I've got to work,' I said lamely. Up to then, I had only half believed tales of what horrible things could happen to adolescent boys. 'We're not allowed in the cellar.'

'Cobblers.'

We reached the cellar. He opened the door, pushed me in, closed it behind him and switched on the light.

'Look, boy. Up here.'

Under a staircase was a mass of white fur. It was several inches deep – nearly a foot in places – and every filament gleamed damply in the light. In the centre of the mass was a bulbous growth looking like an off-coloured mushroom. '*Aspergillus lacrimans*,' he said, with as much reverance as a young pioneer on his first visit to Lenin's tomb. 'Isn't she a beauty?'

'What is it?' I was revolted by the sight and keen to get back to my study.

'I told you, *Aspergillus lacrimans*. Dry rot to you and me.'

'It looks pretty wet to me,' I said. 'Besides, *lacrimans* means weeping, doesn't it?'

'Ah. That's the whole point,' he said. 'This is only the bit you can see. The rest of it is in the wood.'

'In the wood?'

'That's right. The whole staircase is riddled with it. Could give way at any moment.'

'But these are the housemaster's private stairs.'

'Ooh ah.'

'I, er, I suppose you'll have to report it,' I said wistfully. The prospect of my housemaster crashing through the stairs into the cellar, his gown flying behind him like Superman, was palpably delicious.

''Course. S'dangerous.'

It is not difficult to learn to recognise the symptoms of dry rot. The most obvious, where you are looking at a house you've just bought and are having assessed for likely repair costs, is a triumphant grin on your builder's face. Next to subsidence, dry rot is the most lucrative problem a builder can find. Other symptoms are, for example, going to bed on the first floor and waking up with a start on the ground floor, still in bed. Guests or family members suddenly shrinking to half their normal height, chair legs plunging through floors and door knockers going right through the door are other signs.

Dry rot's cousin, and almost as deadly, is wet rot. If you can pick up lumps of your timberwork and wring them out, you have wet rot. The way to prevent this is to keep the wood dry. That way, you'll get only dry rot. When looking at your paintwork, it

It is not difficult to learn to recognise the symptoms
of dry rot.

pays to stick a penknife blade or screwdriver end into the wood. If the blade of your knife meets firm resistance and closes on your hand, cutting your finger, your timber is sound. Now, off you go to the hospital to get your hand stitched up. Oh, didn't you realise your local town hospital casualty department works only nine to five, Monday to Friday. Well, this is the country and you wanted to live here. You have a fifty-mile round trip to your county capital ahead of you now. You must try to remember not to have accidents at the weekend in future! If the knife sinks half-way up its blade into the wood (not into you), you have a mild wet-rot problem. If the knife blade and your fist both sink into the timber, you are in real trouble. But whatever you do, don't panic. Remember, builders make their fortunes out of punter panic. It's a very emotional thing, having the roof over your head threatened, and you can easily work yourself into a psychological state in which you would happily sacrifice your last penny as long as your home is sound. This is what builders rely on.

Animals without Backbones

Next up the biological scale of pests come the invertebrates. This group includes worms, millipedes, insects, molluscs and some clergy. The general rule is, the smaller the resident bug, the more deadly it is. A whopping great beetle, shiny and black with pincer-like jaws, will put the wind up you but is unlikely to hurt your building. The tiny furniture beetle, on the other hand, is a deadly home-wrecker, boring little galleries and catacombs in your timber until the whole lot collapses into handfuls of dust. Moths are the same. A thundering great hawkmoth with a four-inch wingspan and caterpillars the size of chipolatas is completely harmless, but find a centimetre-long insignificant little grey moth in your wardrobe and you'd better hope the punk fashion is here to stay. Clothes moths dislike sweaters from jumble sales or cheap items from discount stores but love cashmere overcoats. The traditional method of moth eradication is to fill the pockets of your best woollens with naphtha mothballs. This makes them smell disgusting – you can always tell a clothes moth victim at a party: she's the one on the far side of the room with nobody less than ten paces away from her – and doesn't always work. Well, I suppose they do keep the party pests at bay.

Cockroaches are dear little things. They have long, wavy antennae and are far too shy to come out during the day. Having an infestation of them says much about you as a housekeeper! In your country home, if it's more than 100 years old, they will not appear, because they rely on warmth. However, if you double glaze and insulate, and your habits are somewhat short of clinical, you might expect an outbreak from time to time, especially after the full effects of insulation have begun to take effect and the wet/dry rot gets properly set in. When you find your first cockroach, don't feel guilty or ashamed. It could happen to anyone! Just go along to your nearest pest-control centre and get the problem seen to by a professional. They are quite unshockable at these places and, to preserve your anonymity, they give you a number and need never know your name. And don't think they'll lecture you on morality – they won't – but do be sure to get the matter cleared up as soon as possible, because it can get a lot worse quite quickly.

The worst, absolutely the worst, insect pest is the deathwatch beetle. A deathwatch beetle can live happily in one of your four-teenth-century oak beams for nearly a decade, just nibbling a bit of wood from time to time to keep the pangs of hunger at bay, until suddenly, after all that inactivity, he feels the urge to pro-create coming on. And not very long after that, following a series of unsung miracles of nature, this very same beam has 21,000 deathwatch beetles all munching through oceans of timber. Within a short time, all that is left of the beam is a pile of powder.

You will know when you have deathwatch beetle. Either the beams in your period residence will be broken or, if the infestation is in the early stages, at dead of night you'll hear an irregular ticking sound. Just remember that for every beetle you hear tick-ing, there are 1,000 others sleeping away their pre-pubertal lives. At the worst possible moment – when the Stock Market has just crashed and you're about to sell up, for example – they will all wake up simultaneously so as to be ready to greet your house buyer's surveyor.

Mortar bees who come home to find their front doors
concreted over take exception.

Mortar bees are only a problem if you have soft mortar. The first indication of the problem is falling masonry. They go in and out through tiny holes but behind the stonework they will have created galleries on a par with the Cheddar caves. They look like friendly bumble bees but don't be fooled. They'll reduce your house to rubble in no time. The remedy is to have the brick or stonework repointed. This takes ages and costs a bomb but it does work. Just stay indoors for six months after the repointing is finished. Mortar bees who come home to find their front doors cemented over take exception and are likely to mob any human within half a mile.

Freelance Experts

When you move into your country home, you'll soon find out that your neighbours are all experts on pest control and pest biology, so free advice will flow copiously from all sides. People who have come from town will be sympathetic and helpful, basing their counsel on their own experiences. Locals will be infuriating. They'll practically queue up to tell you the worst about every aspect of your property and constitute a pretty serious pest problem in themselves. They invariably approach with an 'I-know-something-you-don't-know' air and offer spurious advice in the hopes that you will be mug enough to act on it, hence entertaining all the other locals for ages. Such help usually comes from a conversation in the pub or may drift over the hedge as the local passes by and spots you in the garden. You may have made a big success of your professional career so far but he, though he may be only a farm worker, is a fount of useful knowledge, an expert in everything.

'Good morning to you,' you might say, straightening up from your weeding. 'Lovely day!'

'Swallers are flying high!'

'Yes. They seem to be catching those bees going in and out of our stonework, but aren't they swifts?'

'Whaa? Fast, you mean? Yer, they're swift all right.'

'No. I mean aren't the birds called swifts? Chocolatey brown all over, aren't they?'

'Black.'

'Oh?'

'Swallers're black.'

'Really? I thought they had rusty red throats.'

'Bit of a bird fancier, are yer?'

'Well, one takes an interest.'

'Plenty o' swallers hereabouts.'

'Yes. And swifts and house martins.'

'Ha! You *are* a bird fancier. Good job 'n' all.'

'Oh? Why's that?'

'Crows. In yer roof. You'll know what to do about 'em.'

'Crows?'

'In yer chimneys. There's two up there now. On yer chimney pot. Niver 'ave a fire now, yer won't.'

'We plan to sweep the chimney when the young jackdaws have flown.'

'Niver! Won't do no good.'

'Why?'

'Mortar's knackered. Besides, once them crows come, yer fire never draws again.'

'What about lining the chimney?'

'Niver work. What you want is one o' them nice Rayburns.'

'In the sitting room? It's an inglenook fireplace!'

'Ha! 'ad them cream tiles took out, 'ave yer? Yer'll be sorry yer did that.'

'Why's that?'

'I told yer. It'll niver draw. That's why old Dora put 'em in just after the war. Come winter, you'll see. That's the trouble with this 'ouse. None o' the fires draw. That's why no one round 'ere would buy it. That 'n' the price. Some folks must 'ave more money 'n sense. Then there's the beerbine.'

'Sorry?'

'Beerbine. Yer can't grow anything in the garden. Soil's full of beerbine. Ain't nothin' yer can do about that either.'

'Beerbine?'

'Ah!'

'What does it look like?'

'You'll find out soon enough! 'course, yer soil's worn out too.
Dora never put nuffink back – all them years. That don't help,
but yer could do something about that.'

'Like what? Composting? Mulches? Manure?'

'Ha!'

'Any other ideas?'

'We-ell, they do say old car tyres.'

'I beg your pardon?'

'Yeah. Spread a few old tyres around. It's the rubber – draws
up the green. I'll tell the lads ter drop a tyre or two over yer
'edge when I go down the pub if yer like.'

At this point, unless you react firmly, you'll have sixty car tyres
thrown over your hedge within a week. These will attract other
rubbish and life won't be worth living.

'No thank you. No tyres.'

'Suit yourself. Yer won't be gardening 'ere long anyway.'

'Why not?'

'I told yer. Beerbine!'

It's the kind of conversation to drive you to drink. In fact,
you've wasted so much time now you might as well go and sink
a pint of wallop in the pub. At least it'll be real ale, kept just for
the likes of you – indigenous locals drink draft lager, except on
Saturdays, when they drink draft lager until they can't get any
more down and then they go on to rum and peppermint until they
can't stand up, after which, because they can still sit, they drive
home. Though you've been into the pub fourteen times in the last
month, the landlord greets you as a total stranger.

'Good evening, sir!'

'Good evening, er, Fred,' you reply. You order your real ale
and, turning to take your glass to the table by the window, notice,
with a sinking feeling, that your earlier acquaintance is in the
corner with two of his cronies.

''ullo, given it up already?' he asks. Then, turning to his neighbour, a wizened relic who looks as though he should be wearing
a smock, says, 'Gennelman what's got old Dora's place.'

'Huh,' wheezes the relic. 'Good luck to 'n.'

The other crony, in a stage whisper, says: 'Knows about the
beerbine, do 'e?'

This causes all shoulders to shake. By now you're feeling a little narked about the attitude, but say nothing, deciding to keep the friendly smile at the ready.

'Any one care for a – ' But before you've finished the sentence, three empty pint glasses have been banged on the counter.

'Lager,' they say, in unison.

'And a bag o' them cheese 'n' onion crisps.'

'Pork scratchings!'

'Gi's a foo peanuts, Fred!' Glasses filled and nibbles distributed, they all look at you. 'Cheers, mate,' they chorus and then go back to their huddle. You strain to hear the conversation but only snippets come forth, punctuated by giggles.

' . . . Dora . . . beerbine – '

' . . . Nearly killed poor old Fred Biggins – '

' . . . Water table . . . stands ter reason – '

' . . . Nar, consumption in them days, wannit? – '

' . . . Niver draw. Too damp, break 'is heart –'

' . . . Beerbine, riddled wi'it – '

' . . . Beam cracked . . . condemned by that council thing – '

' . . . Subsidy – '

' . . . Naow, stoopid sub*sidence* . . . no foundations.'

It doesn't take them long. You gulp the last of your real ale, forgetting to chew the sediment, and bolt for the door. Just as you close it behind you you hear, faintly, 'Like another mate?' followed by a gale of laughter. You feel a little pang, at this stage, for that noisy, friendly little wine bar just off Holborn. Furthermore, the real ale has made you feel sick.

Other people who have themselves moved into the village and surrounding areas from elsewhere will be far more sympathetic. Often their advice comes at parties, or perhaps at your housewarming.

'My dear, I *love* your inglenook. How *did* you find it?'

'Pulled that hideous tile thing out and there it was!'

'Have you lit a fire in it yet?'

'Can't, there's a jackdaw nesting in the chimney pot.'

'Are you sure it's just in the pot, lovey? We thought that at the rectory, but when Rodney went into the roof cavity to find out where the rain was coming in, he found a whole colony. All among the rafters!'

'How lovely!'

'Lovely? My dear it was *ghastly*! Not just jackdaws either. There were starlings and, of all things, bats!'

'Lucky you. I wish we had bats. Our roof's the wrong design. Nowhere for them to get in.'

'Well, if you do get them, for God's sake don't let on. It's illegal to bump them off nowadays. Anyway, if you want to clear the chimney, just light a fire – that'll shift 'em!'

'Not till the fledglings have flown!'

'I say, darling, you're not one of these Greens, are you?'

'Well. That's sort of, more or less, why we came to live in the country. You know, nature and all that.'

'Good heavens. Rodney, darling! Come over here. We've got a Green in our midst!'

'Well, isn't that why you came here?'

'Hell, no, darling. We sold our house in Twickenham for half a mill and got the rectory for 100 K. Complete ruin, of course, but say no more! We're using the income from the balance to finance the renovations.'

'Does it cover the costs?'

'Sort of. Well. It helps. But look. I'll tell you how we keep those bloody jackdaws away from the chimney. Rodney's got this amazing gadget you plug in. It makes a high-pitched scream which they can hear but we humans can't. Isn't that clever!'

'Does it scare away other birds?'

'Yes, everything. It's absolutely marvellous! Ah, here's Rodney.'

Garden Pests

Growing your own food provides all manner of pests with a heaven-sent opportunity to plague your life. The worst of these menaces are gardening experts, but if you want sound advice on how to deal with such people – and there is a world surplus of them – you'd better get hold of a copy of this book's companion volume, *This Gardening Business*. As far as pest control in the kitchen garden is concerned, you have two choices: starve or use chemicals. Organic gardening is for ideals, not for food. Sometimes those who move into the country and start growing their own food decide to go organic. They don't necessarily go the whole hog, donning hair shirts or turning up at the shops in clothing they wove themselves out of shredded birch twigs and wild flax, but they do decide to eat only food which is totally uncontaminated by artificial fertiliser, pesticide or Common Market legislation. Before long, they discover why organic produce looks so scabby. Short of creeping up on the pests with a mallet, you have nothing with which to combat them. Every greenfly, cabbage white, carrotfly, cutworm, eelworm, thrips (one thrips, many thrips, there's no such thing as a thrip), scaly bug, red spider mite, wireworm, slug and snail within a dozen miles soon hears on the grapevine, apple tree, raspberry cane or whatever plant they happen to be desecrating at the time that yet another townee has moved in, locked the chemical store door and thrown away the key. Before your young vegetable seedlings have even managed to put a tentative leaf out into the world, they are there, munching, sucking juices, scabbing surfaces and holing foliage until your vegetable plot looks as though a chemical defoliant has been used. But don't let this depress you. At least the single wizened apple and the three spotty potatoes you carry to the house, wrapped in a cabbage leaf peppered with slug holes and streaked with dwarfing virus, are pure and wholesome.

Worse, oh far worse, than growing organically yourself is having a productive kitchen garden but organic neighbours. If, as so often happens, they happen to have strong political views as well and are inclined to be crusaders, you have indeed a heavy cross to bear. Whenever they look over the fence and see you scattering a little ammonium nitrate or spraying your roses for aphids, their tongues will click reproachfully, but how often will they be round for a bunch of leeks or a basket of apples when their own crops fail? Naturally, while they are helping themselves to your fruits, they will give you the benefit of their opinions on everything from the advance of AIDS to the decline of the common bat.

'OO-ooh! Alison! Hi! How are you?'

'Jolyon! When did you arrive? Has Annabelle come down with you?'

'Half an hour ago. Yes. Thanks for keeping an eye on the place. Great weather, isn't it? Such a relief to be out of London. The fumes!'

'I'm afraid the caterpillars have rather done for your greens. Did you do anything about them before you left?'

'We're growing penstemons between the rows. The colours of the flowers are supposed to confuse the butterflies so that they lay their eggs on the wrong plants and the caterpillars die of starvation.'

'Doesn't seem to have worked. We use Dimethoate to kill them off in our patch.'

'Ah, but think of the damage you're doing to the environment. And to yourselves, of course.'

'I'm sure you're right but you may have to buy your lunch anyway. Your potatoes have got blight and your peas don't look too healthy.'

'Buy? What? Where?'

'Well, lettuce, cabbages and things.'

'We can't possibly. There isn't a wholefood shop in Crudchester and I'm blowed if I'm driving all the way to Lymeswold Minster just for food.'

'What's wrong with our greengrocer?'

'What's wrong? They have South African apples, that's what's wrong.'

'Well, you could specify English produce. I'm sure they'll have it.'

'Provide those Lincolnshire farmers with more Mercs and BMWs, you mean? Do you know just how much subsidy they get? That's taxes, my money and your money stolen out of our own pockets.'

'Actually, we manage to produce our own veg and most of our own fruit, but I suppose you won't want these mangetouts I've just picked, or this lovely crisp Cos lettuce, or this basket of new potatoes. Pity, I'd even picked a sprig of mint for you to boil with them.'

'Oh really? Oh well, actually, I know how careful you are with your sprays and things, so I think we could stretch a point this time, er, thanks.'

'Don't mench.'

'I say, while you've got that basket handy, how about a few strawberries, broad beans and asparagus?'

The other form of human pest which can cause untold damage to your pocket as well as to your nerves is the tenant. You may find that you need to vacate your country home for a while and, thinking it will do the house good to be lived in during your absence, you decide to let it for the duration of your stay away. Fatal! Ah, you might say, but we can go for good tenants. But what you probably don't realise is that the better educated and more affluent your tenants, the more damage they'll do. Leave a pretty cottage in someone else's care and you're sure to come home to a tatty wreck with a garden full of weeds and a house with cracks in the windows and layers of burnt grime on the cooker. The children will have done art work with wax crayons all over the walls and the best curtains will have a huge stain of blue dye right in the middle.

'Oh, that's where little Fafner threw his felttip at Freya. Luckily it missed her but sort of got wedged in a curtain and all the ink soaked out.'

If you start remonstrating about things, your tenants are likely to retaliate with a list of defects.

'Did you realise the loo blocks so easily? We had to get Draina-poke in three times; they'll be sending you a bill. Freya's teddy got down there once, but it shouldn't really have blocked just because of that. Two rings on the cooker don't work. They bust just after you left, but must have been on the point of going for ages. Oh yes, the Best Kept Village committee have been round twice. They say your front garden's a disgrace and something will have to be done about it before judging next week or you will be blamed for ruining their chances this year. By the way, that magnolia tree has some kind of rot, because when we fixed Fafner's swing to it it just snapped and fell over. I think that's all. Oh no, one more thing, there's water dripping into the wall just below the eaves. I suspect it comes out of an overflow or something, but we thought it better not to interfere. It means the wall in the guestroom has gone very green and slimy and the windowsill has rotted. We could hardly put guests in there now, so lately we've been putting them up at the pub. I expect you'll be able to knock a bit off the rent, though, won't you?'

The one good thing about having tenants is that they cure you of ever wanting to do home swap holidays. In theory, two like-minded families from similar income groups swap homes for a couple of weeks. Thus if you live near, say, Winchester, you could swap with some Americans who might live somewhere pretty like Watkins Glen. Before you leave, you stock the fridge to the gunwhales with especially English goodies, like game pie, sausages and farmhouse cheese, and make sure there are vast quantities of food in the pantry, together with lists of suppliers of milk, groceries and meat and telephone numbers of local doctor, plumber, dentist and so on. Naturally, you make sure the house is cleaner that it has ever been and, by way of a fairly broad hint, you leave a box of cleaning materials out on the dresser.

At Watkins Glen, before you can start your holiday, you have to clean up and stock the house you are borrowing. Since your plane was late into Kennedy and since you missed your connecting flight, it was nearly midnight before you discovered the small, wooden hut by Lake Seneca that you had swapped for your lovely sixteenth-century farmhouse. The Americans, it seems, use it only as a weekend retreat and furthermore, judging by the absence of anything edible, the broken gas stove and the sock hanging from the light socket in the tiny living room, these retreats are infrequent but frenetic when they happen. You spend your holiday worrying about what they are doing to your home in England, not to mention your reputation.

When you return, the only thing undisturbed is the box of cleaning materials you left on the dresser. The refrigerator is empty except for what appears to be the mate of the sock which hung on the Watkins Glen light fitting. There is a pile of lager tins outside which threatens to dwarf Mont Blanc and your Marc Chagall print has gone missing. When you go outside to empty the overflowing and stinking kitchen bin, you see a near neighbour walking up the street. In response to your cheerful greeting, he sniffs and turns tail. Oh dear, you are going to be unpopular. Whatever did the Americans get up to? You find out months later, when the neighbours begin to talk to you again.

Now that you have a deep and thorough knowledge of every kind of household pest, do you feel able to cope with life in an old country house? Before moving to the next chapter, just brush up your knowledge with the following.

1 Can you identify any of the following?
(a) *Xenopsylla cheopsis,* (b) a katydid, (c) a whatkatydidnext, (d) a furniture beetle, (e) an Ombudsman, (f) a cockchafer, (g) a paycock.

2 If you see any of them in your home, what should you do?
(a) Call the police, (b) stamp them out on your own, (c) learn to appreciate their points of view and share your life with them?

3 Rank the following pests in order of importance:
(a) Children, (b) moulds, (c) insects, (d) neighbourhood watch schemes, (e) Jehovah's Witnesses, (f) mortar bees, (g) rats.

4 Which of the following is odd one out?
(a) Dry rot expert, (b) gardening expert, (c) local government pest-control officer, (d) agricultural pesticide consultant.

5 Which species of bat can you destroy without being prosecuted?

Answers

2 None of these, but prepare for plague, structural collapse and an infestation of Irish and American literature.

3 All come first equal.

4 (c) All the rest actually control pests.

5 A cricket bat.

Chapter 9

A Concise History of Architecture

Those who have no artificial means of ascertaining the progress of time, are in general the most acute in discerning its immediate signs.

(William Hazlitt, *On a Sundial*, 1827)

The most important point to remember about British architecture is that it doesn't exist. There is, quite simply, no such animal. All we have ever had is a hotch-potch of weird continental ideas, adapted for British use. Since the Second World War, this jumble of rehashed classical or Gothic styles has rubbed shoulders uneasily with modern creations of concrete, glass and mangled metal.

In this chapter we will attempt to trace the development of architecture, from the crude brushwood huts of the Neolithic to the crude brushwood huts of today's 'starter home' developments. Luckily for you, unlike a qualified architectural historian, I am able to give you a fully objective and completely logical account. We will have no need to concern ourselves with dry technicalities but instead can cast our critical eyes down the pages of history and see what *they*, the experts, have imposed on us, the customers.

There are, say the experts, two main kinds of building: power architecture and vernacular building. Power architecture really means stately homes – buildings designed not for comfortable living but to show the peasantry who was in charge. Banks, department stores, factories and bus stations are modern examples. Vernacular building is what most of us live in today – erected by peasants for mortgagees. But before we get into any serious discussion, we should first glance down the short glossary of architectural terms which follows. Familiarising yourself with these words will enable you to get the maximum benefit from all the learned material this chapter contains.

Andirons Metal fire-dogs with round knobs on them for warming the 'ands.

Baluster From the Greek *Balaustion* a pomegranate?! Like trouser or scissor, pretty useless on its own. Stood in rows, it makes a balustrade.

Basilica A domestic item, usually of earthenware, designed to germinate basil seeds during cold weather.

Bressummer More accurately breastsummer – a wide, load-bearing lintel useful for taking exercise or to hang people from.

Cantilever The correct technical name for a tin opener.

Clerestory A form of narrative without symbolism or hidden meanings of any kind but always bearing a moral and punchline. Roald Dahl is said to be the greatest living writer of clerestories.

Cloisters The most expensive ski resort in Europe.

Cob A male mute swan. Distinguishable by the enlarged black knob on its bill and its foul temper.

Corbel The bit of stone which pokes out from a wall and supports a beam end and which, if you are lucky enough to miss the beam, you bang your head on.

Cornice Ice cream served in a conical wafer.

Dowels Faces on clocks, circular arrangements of numbers on telephones, etc (cf. Dowelling tone, Dowel a recipe, etc.).

Dressed stone Building material coated with oil and vinegar – to prolong its life, presumably.

Earth closet A small cupboard or enclosure for storing potting compost, peat and horticultural sundries.

Finial The architect's last word on his building.

Flying buttresses American aircraft used in the Second World War for saturation bombing of the enemy.

Geodesic A veterinary cure for such animal diseases as portland bill, beachy head, chep's toe and stow-on-the-wold.

Gothic (Originally Goethic) nineteenth-century architecture derived from early church styles where gloomy, arch-shaped windows made interiors dark and depressing.

Grotto A hole or cave in a large garden designed for holding rubbish – hence 'grotty' and 'grot'.

Lintel An international telecommunications company based in Lincolnshire.

Mullions Callouses or sores suffered by stonemasons who specialise in the fine stonework surrounding window-frames.

Palladian A common name for theatres: for example, the London Palladian.

Pantheon Technical name for saucepan cupboard.

Pendentive construction Building designed so that one part depends on the next for support. Pull out the wrong pillar and the entire building collapses. Never attempt DIY in a pendentive house.

Rotunda A health farm for overweight businessmen.

Spandrels Footwear made from woven leather thongs which are wound round the ankles and calves in a criss-cross pattern (*see* Shakespeare's *Twelfth Night*, 'Wherefore art thou spandrelled, good Malvolio?').

Threshold A form of tenancy (cf. Leasehold, Freehold, Stranglehold, etc.).

Transept A point where one motorway or railway crosses another.

Truss A support for hernia sufferers.

Undercroft The subtext of an estate agent's narrative – that part which is not printed but is clearly understood by the reader from inuendo. For example, Text: 'An important nineteenth-century Gothic structure'; undercroft: 'An ugly Victorian building in red brick with windows like churches'.

Vault An unpleasant disease, common in medieval times, affecting skin, joints and, in extreme cases, the wallet. (Commonest forms: Groin Vault and Rib Vault, caused by living in damp buildings, and Barrel Vault, caused by excessive drinking.)

Looking at the origins of mankind, it's difficult to decide just where architecture began and the troglodytic existence ceased.

Once the caves were full up, the overspill population had to move into the open. This was no fun at all, especially if you lived north of Watford, and living beneath the shelter of handy trees and shrubs was scarcely any better. Careful study, by the academics of the time, of the resources available to them revealed that they had a surplus of mud and not much else. Mud was cheap, untaxed, malleable, biodegradable, caused no damage to the ozone layer and could be remodelled into something bigger and better after every rainfall. It was good for the complexion too. Enter, therefore, the golden age – or more precisely, the dark-brown age – of the mud hut, and very successful it was too, lasting in one form or another for thousands of years. Permanence came to the individual mud hut, much as it did later to the individual fruit pie so beloved of contemporary builders, when it was discovered that the right kind of mud could be cooked into bricks. And still the best houses are built of bricks and not, as architects would until recently have preferred us to believe, of prefabricated plastic, steel and concrete.

The Greeks, however, built their mud huts out of stone. Then they hit on the idea of having two uprights of stone, called columns, with another bit of stone across the top. We can see something similar at Stonehenge, but the Greeks used softer stone, which they could carve into fluted columns decorated with tufts of acanthus leaves, Greek builders being of an aesthetic disposition and prone to making lifestyle statements bold enough to last thousands of years. They had not yet been corrupted, you understand, by individual fruit pies. Having got that far, knocking up the Parthenon was a doddle. Great architecture had arrived, and how.

After the Greeks came the Romans. They copied everything Greek, changing the names slightly to avoid infringing patents and copyright laws. Thus, Heracles became Hercules, Odysseus became Ulysses and Attic wine gave way to Frascati. Virgil cribbed the best Greek poems and everybody forgot the importance of the Greek philosophers, but whenever a new building project was started members of the Roman royal family complained unless the new architecture was of a 'traditional', that is Greek, nature. However, one new technique, the arch, was introduced by Rome and this was to revolutionise everything. Not only did it allow comfortable passage to obese Roman dignitaries – the Romans were great ones for overindulgence – it could also bear heavy loads, and very soon the arch became the universal feature of an ever more adventurous architecture. Arches have been lengthened into vaults, used as bridges, used for underground railways, made into aqueducts and even carry sewers. Since early Christian times, they have played a key role in church architecture, particularly in cathedrals, which were the first buildings to have special clergy appointed to maintain them – archbishops. But, with the arch, architectural development pretty well stopped. All that followed was little more than embellishment or refinement. St Paul's Cathedral, for example, is merely a refined Roman temple, as are Chartres, Versailles and the Leicester Square Odeon.

By the time the Romans had colonised England, they were in serious decline. They had inflation, unemployment, a disintegration in moral values, a corrupt and violent police force and the most appalling pornography problem. In fact, the empire was subsiding into one prolonged orgy; but not in England, partly because it was far too cold and partly because everybody was more concerned about the Lagerlout invasions threatened from Denmark and Norway. Terrifying warriors who were covered in flax-coloured hair but wore very little else, despite the cruelly cold climate of their homeland, would deliver barrels of urine-coloured beer to the coastal villages and then withdraw until the inhabitants had drunk themselves into a stupor. At that point, the rape and pillage began and lasted until the Norman invasion of 1066. In all those years, nobody had thought of building fortified houses or castles to repel the Lagerlouts, but they did pass licensing laws which forbade the drinking of the beer at certain times of the day.

The chief organiser of the Norman invasion was a man called William. He was an estate agent obsessed with title deeds. As soon as he had established his first UK office, conveniently sited in the Home Counties near Hastings, he began to compile a vast book containing particulars of every choice property in the land. The population of England worshipped him because of his invaluable research, and that's how we became a nation of property owners – or some of us did anyway. His method was quite simple. When his surveyors fanned out across the land they noted down all the buildings. Wretched mud hovels were ignored and left to the peasantry, but anything approaching desirability was simply transferred to his ownership and subsequently leased back to a deserving baron. (Deserving meant Norman. Saxons were either killed or sent to the Isle of Ely; most opted for death.)

William began the trend in country houses, which continues today, of building for grandeur and strength rather than for comfort. Gentlemen's houses were vast, but the peasantry were expected to carry on living in upturned coracles or crude brushwood huts. William's son Rufus took over the family estate agency business and had the ridiculous idea of pulling down all recent developments in Hampshire and planting a new green belt, hoping thereby to win the affection of the muesli and sandal brigade. Enraged at being dispossessed of their homes and farms, the Hampshirites murdered him in the middle of his New Forest and from that point on, all successors of the original Norman conquests went completely paranoid and built themselves freezing-cold, draughty castles with glassless windows and unscalable walls. The idea was to make such places so uncomfortable that nobody in their right mind would want to invade them. To this day, stately homes are excessively cold and inconvenient. Meanwhile, the peasantry still starved in pitiful hovels.

Then came the Wars of the Roses, followed by the Renaissance. This was the dawning of an age of enlightenment. Stately homes were still as draughty and inconvenient as before, but they got larger and so it was an even longer walk to the bathroom. The fortifications – battlements, inner bailies, outer bailies, bill bailies and so on – gradually gave way to landscaped gardens and parterres, so defence gave way to swank. This made it easy for Oliver Cromwell, the advance guard of the Labour Party, to win the Civil War. However, he was so disastrous at organising a monarchless Britain that in the end people had to beg the Royals to come back and carry on being dissolute and irresponsible as before. During all this time, the peasantry was still floundering around up to their naughty bits in muck and still living in dismal hovels.

Later, when Queen Anne failed to provide an heir, Parliament invited an arrogant, disinterested German to rule the nation. George and his successors had one aim in life – to keep all the peasants in hovels but at the same time to make sure there was no nonsense like a French-style revolution. George ruled with a rod of iron – still called Black Rod to this day and waved about at the State Opening of Parliament. In 1790 you could be hanged for almost every offence, from regicide to parking your carriage on a double yellow. Nobody staged a French revolution in England after all, but although the British began their war with France because they disagreed with such democratic principles, by the time they had finished they were fighting the kind of tyranny in Napoleon that they had championed in the French royal family.

What England did have was an Industrial Revolution. The peasants – crushed and suppressed since the Peasant Revolt in 1381 – at last rose in a body. The revolution was a resounding success and within a trice the peasants had deserted their rude hovels and become factory workers. Their average life expectancy leapt from twenty-nine to thirty-one, their wages rocketed from a shilling a week to one and a penny and everyone was well satisfied, in spite of the carpings of a handful of busybodies calling themselves Whigs, Reformers and Philanthropists.

The most important architectural development to come out of the Industrial Revolution was the slum. After forsaking their country dwellings, the peasants needed housing which would enable them to enjoy a certain lifestyle but which, though an improvement on the rude hovels, would still not be too grand and therefore make them feel uncomfortable. Mill owners thoughtfully supplied the average family of ten – there was no contraception in those days – with two-bedroomed houses, built back to back with a street in the middle for the sewage to run down and the youngest children to play in. To help with the problems of overcrowding, they allowed children to work in the mills or down the mines, so that there were fewer people at home during the day.

Slums have continued to be the chief style of housing in urban areas. Different shapes of slum have emerged from time to time. Stacking them in piles and calling them tower blocks was popular in the post-war years, but the occupants of these revolutionary buildings were unhappy about not having gardens. There was nowhere for the children to play and, since the lifts kept going wrong, old people frequently found themselves with several hundred steps to climb. Lower groups of slums were built with interconnecting balconies and small play areas for children, but these caused a rise in crime and none of the mothers dared risk the lives of their children in the play areas, where child molesters, muggers and German Shepherd dogs lurked ready to pounce on their victims. The trend has tended to be to revert to the original back-to-back type of slum, but these days those that don't belong to local councils are being bought at inflated prices by stock-brokers and City analysts.

That really brings us up to the present day. The ex-peasants still live in slums, the aristocracy still have their freezing stately homes and the parliamentarians are as ineffectual and mendacious as ever. However, there is one really huge difference between today and the Georgian era. Today we have the Great Middle Class. I don't want to be presumptious and please don't be cross if I'm wrong, but I suspect that this means you!

The problem with the middle class has always been that they look down on the peasants, from whom they have risen, but rather envy their moral lassitude. At the same time, they try to imitate the aristocracy, even though they despise them as well. Thus middle-class people assess each other in the most pecular ways. Anyone who owns a car more than four years old is judged a failure, but he who drives something overtly vulgar, like a Porsche or a Mercedes, is guilty of that unforgivable crime, swanking. One needs a vehicle which is clearly expensive but so inelegant and so unimaginative in its design that nobody could possibly accuse its owner of trying to cut a dash – a Volvo, perhaps, or a large Ford. As for correct behaviour, eating fish and chips out of newspaper in the street is considered unseemly but eating asparagus with a fork instead of your fingers is beyond the pale. Vowel sounds which smack of the proletariat or drinking coffee out of mugs, especially with the milk bottle on the table, all have bad vibes for middle-class folk, but then so do mink coats, high heels before breakfast and wearing ties for Sunday lunch.

With all those mores pulling in different directions, it's not surprising that middle-class architecture turns out to be a hybrid between the stately home and the peasant hovel. The middle-class house in the country is usually a stately home in microcosm but with a few creature comforts thrown in. There are certain features common to all, regardless of when the house was built and by whom.

A mower shed. One of the great horticultural fallacies is that grass is easier to manage than a proper garden. Since the 1950s, most country-house owners have done away with their flowerbeds and turned their entire gardens over to lawn and trees. The result is that they now spend every waking hour in the summer fighting a losing battle with the grass, which seems to grow faster every year, and with their lawnmowers, which become more sophisticated but less reliable and less efficient at grass cutting every year.

A utility room. The euphemism for 'punitive labour department'. Since all country houses are designed for containing one family, one housekeeper, one cook, one butler and three maids, and since the most you can expect these days is a grumpy individual who will break the Hoover and read all your mail for two hours a week, it follows that most of the work which used to be done by those six retainers will be done by you.

An outsized chimney void. This is what you find when curiosity gets the better of you and you try to find out what goes on in that twenty feet of unaccounted space between the bedroom wall and the guest bathroom. You knock a stone or two out to make a hole, only to find that there is an ancient fireplace there, full of jackdaws' nests, cobwebs and soot, most of which falls out on to your new carpet.

A fancy front door which nobody uses. All grand country homes have an incredibly posh front door which is never opened. Strangers ring bells and strike door knockers in vain because everyone else knows that if that door were ever to be opened, the whole west elevation would sag half an inch and the door would never be closed again.

An inconvenient garage. One cannot order one's carriage for three o'clock these days. Good country houses have stables which are miles away, downwind of the residential parts, and besides, they've usually been converted into houses. Garages built conveniently near the house ruin the looks of the place or are simply not allowed because of the house being a listed building, so either your car lives al fresco or you need hiking boots for the trip to the garage.

Crunchy gravel. No country house can ever be surrounded by anything else. It gets in the Hoover, it is agony in open-toed sandals and weeds grow in it with gay abandon, but what else could you possibly have? Tarmac? I say, really??!! What did they have before gravel was invented? Why, mud and farm animals, of course.

A kitchen garden. This is not, as you might have thought, a place to provide food for the house. It is in reality a walled-off area full of weeds and broken cucumber frames where children play hide-and-seek and where washing can be hung out to be rained on.

Blocked-in windows. They'll tell you that these were blocked in because of the window tax in the eighteenth century. Don't you believe it! The windows will have been blocked in because the house was subsiding and the glass kept cracking. Replace the bricked-in areas with glass at your peril!

A wine cellar. This is in the bowels of the house and is used to store jumble-sale items which nobody bought, old school trunks covered in mould, last year's Christmas tree decorations, a flattened mouse and half a bottle of home-made elderflower wine which is so acid it has begun to dissolve the glass itself.

Our Architectural Heritage

Before moving on from this chapter, we ought to be familiar with the more prominent of the architects who have added their own little quirks and foibles to the Graeco-Roman buildings that have been copied all over Europe.

Adam, Robert The first-ever architect. In fact, the first-ever person. Known for his originality, which is not surprising considering his chronology. Inclined to be influenced by women.

Bakewell, Robert Inventor of a tart with almond-flavoured filling and raspberry jam.

Bell, Henry Seventeenth-century campanologist who designed the famous Bell Tower at King's Lynn before going to Scotland to open a whisky distillery.

Brown, Capability An eighteenth-century vandal who destroyed perfectly good gardens to make room for horrid, butyl-lined ponds and heaps of earth supposedly looking like natural hills but all terribly, terribly bogus.

Le Courbusier A brand of Cognac.

Lutyens, Edwin The greatest creator of modern copies of old buildings. His modern copies of old buildings made India look like Tunbridge Wells.

Gibbons, Grinling A woodcarver who wrote the critically acclaimed eighteenth-century thriller *The Rise and Fall of the Roman Reich.*

Jekyll, Gertrude Garden designer whose alter ego designed Hyde Park. Famous for her quip, 'A rose is a rose is a rose.'

Jones, Inigo Eighteenth-century architect famous especially for doorways. Known in his native Wales as 'Jones the Door'.

Keep, Norman The twelfth-century castle architect who originated the idea of glassless windows to discourage invaders.

Kent, William An architect and landscape designer so famous he had a whole county named after him.

Palumbo, P. An American television series about a shabby, boss-eyed detective. (Not to be confused with Christopher Palumbo, who discovered the West Indies in 1492.)

Romanesque Czechoslovakian architect of the twelfth century who specialised in rounded arches.

Timbers, Shivermy Little is known about this architect who specialised in using structural sections of old sailing ships for fishermen's cottages in Wales.

Vanbrugh, John Eighteenth-century inventor of life assurance and commercial vehicles.

Wren, Christopher One of our greatest architects – i.e. better at copying classic Italian design than most. Famous for using work as an excuse for dodging social commitments – 'if anyone calls, say I'm designing St Paul's' – when he was really chasing crumpet in Vauxhall Gardens.

The Future

What will happen next? Well, one thing is for sure: there won't be much countryside left. What with twentieth-century agriculture doing away with hedges and woods, soon there'll be nowhere for us honest country folk to dump our rubbish. There won't be much space left if you urbanites insist on building your executive villas in our villages, just because you can't find any period properties which are far enough away from the railway, aerodrome, sewage works, missile site, A1, M6, etc. or which don't cost £750,000. Then there's the decline in services to worry about. Once British Rail has been privatised it will close its last half-dozen rural stations. The new private water companies will find it unprofitable to pipe water to outlying hamlets, so, just as they can't get gas today, by the year 2000 they won't have water or electricity either.

As for houses, well, sooner or later somebody's got to explode this ridiculous myth which the countryside has become and build sensibly. Editors of country magazines – elegant ladies who inhabit space-age offices in the heart of rustic Westminster – are in part responsible for what has become a great British love affair but which, like so many whirlwind romances, is a mere infatuation. High-profile conservationists, and how few of them actually live in the country, are almost as bad, screaming rape whenever a farmer starts up a hedge trimmer but overlooking the disastrous effect of too many visitors to the more popular nature reserves. When I was a lad, Wicken Fen, where swallowtail butterflies flew, had few visitors and was a mish-mash of narrow paths threading their way through the sedge fen. I went there two years ago and found that those same paths are now twenty feet wide, with much of the vegetation trampled into a quagmire. But enough of this whining! Back to the houses.

They need to be designed for modern living – comfort and convenience first, looks afterwards. Heresy? Not really. Unless we are millionaires, we're unlikely to build anything terribly grand these days, but there is not necessarily any virtue in making all buildings in every village look the same. There's nothing very pretty about a modern house anyway, and if we're forced to have, say, miserably small windows and an awkwardly pitched roof just because the other mean little residences in the village street look like that, then shame on the planners! Let's be bold. Let's put up distinctive properties which are making brave statements for today. The countryside is not a museum, full of antiques to be cherished at any price. It is part of the geography of our everyday lives, so let's live, not for ancient heritage but for today. And let's hand something original and exciting on to our descendants, so that in their future days they will see that we commoners made our mark in the twentieth century.

Here are a few exercises to see how much you've taken in.

1 Where would you find crockets?
(a) On a church door, **(b)** in a motor car showroom, **(c)** in a pinnacle, **(d)** on a bicycle wheel.

2 What is a pompidou?
(a) A famous centre in Paris, **(b)** a method of defining a kind of rhythm – as in pom-pom-pom-pidou, **(c)** a type of archway, **(d)** French for a motor tyre inflator.

3 If a ceiling is embossed, does it mean:
(a) Someone has been put in charge of it, **(b)** it's covered in nobbly bits which act as dust traps, **(c)** that if you give a lecture in a room with such a ceiling everyone will be trying to make out what the shapes on it are and not listening to a word you're saying.

Answers

1 In Old Tennessee.

2 Probably.

3 Yes.

Chapter 10

Moving Out

**Sometimes you hear, fifth hand
As epitaph:**
*He chucked up everything
And just cleared off, . . .*

(Philip Larkin, 'Poetry of Departures')

This is it, then. The crunch. The crisis. Climax to Act Three.
What will you do now that you've decided you hate the country
and long to get back to town? Grin and bear it or unscramble all
you've done and get out while you're still solvent?

If you decide to hang on, you will need vast reserves of moral
fortitude. Things will not get better, because they never do. As
you get older, the inconvenience of the nearest supermarket being
seven miles away, the lack of public transport, the mud and muck
which last from September to May, the dust and flies which last
from June to September, the endless drone of midnight tractors
from August to Christmas, the barrage of guns, hooters and sirens
scaring pigeons off the oilseed rape from Hogmanay to Easter
and the endless carping of the Parochial Church Council will dig
deeper and deeper into your soul until you become as taciturn
and morose as your country neighbours. Culturally, you will dry
up. Even though London is an easy train ride away, organising
everything in advance – lining up someone to feed the dog/cat/
goats/chickens, to water the greenhouse, to check for burst pipes
and cart the children off to school while you are away – is such

an effort that the number of times you go to a theatre, cinema, opera or art gallery will diminish until you reduce yourself to one visit per year. Your brain will be so addled by then that the deepest intellectual exercise possible for you to undertake will be to watch something by Lloyd Webber. People like Ibsen, Marlowe, Britten and Ingmar Bergman are out. You'll never see them performed or screened and your rustic neighbours will think the first is a lavatory cleanser and the last Humphrey Bogart's co-star in *Casablanca* – or will they? Perhaps even *Casablanca* is beyond their ken.

If you decide to get out, your finances are going to be up the spout. You'll never get what you paid for your house, not when you add on all that extra spending you did when you first moved in. Furthermore, town house prices have escalated more sharply than country homes, so you'll lose out that way too. But don't despair. It will be lovely to get back to the smoke, won't it. Fresh food in the shops again, your friends all a short tube ride away, lots to do in the evenings and above all, neighbours who mind their own business! This chapter is designed to help you get the best out of selling your house and to make your return to urban bliss, or elsewhere, as hasty and trouble-free as possible.

Selling Up

Unless you plan to keep it for use as a summer retreat, you'll have to sell the house. There are two possibilities here: using an agent or selling it yourself.

If you do your own selling, you save on the agent's commission. Clever if you know what you're doing, but the pitfalls are horrible. For a start, do you really know the true value of your property? There is a simple formula which estate agents use, based on the number of bedrooms, rateable value and gut feel, but the problem is that even estate agents seldom get it right, so how are mere amateurs expected to arrive at a sensible figure? The true value of any property is defined as **that figure which is actually paid on completion**. In other words, a house is worth exactly what someone is prepared to pay for it. The most crummy, unsound shack with a tin roof could be worth hundreds of thousands if a person happens to want it very badly. One point to bear in mind is that there is no law which says you have to name a price. Just inviting offers could surprise you.

Even if you get the price you want, not having an agent could land you with serious difficulties if you end up with an unprincipled buyer. Agents are usually able to sniff such pests out. They may well have had them through their books before, or at least have heard of them. They know the kind of tricks such people get up to – playing you along until you have committed yourself to buying another house, for example, and then blackmailing you into dropping your price by inventing a bad surveyor's report. They may also consent to certain conditions by 'gentleman's agreement' but renege on those as soon as contracts have been exchanged. This usually applies to little points which, though hardly worth including in the contract, nevertheless matter to you. For example, your apple crop has no commercial value but you'd like permission to come in and pick it when the fruit has ripened, a week or two after completion. The purchaser agrees wholeheartedly with this until you arrive on 20 October with your fruit basket on your arm. You knock at your ex-door. It opens a crack.

'Yes?'

'Ah, hullo Mr Chepeskayt. Settled in all right?'

'Hardly. Did you want something?'

'Just the apples. We agreed – '

'Apples?'

'Yes, you agreed we could pick our crop for the last time.'

'You'll be lucky.'

'Oh?'

'Chopped all the trees down. First thing we did.'

'Oh dear! Are there any apples left on the ground?'

'Plenty.'

'Well, may I pick them up?'

'I don't recommend it. We've sprayed the whole orchard off with paraquat.'

But don't think that selling through agents will be plain sailing. They have the strangest foibles. The first is a complete U-turn from the policy they seemed to have had when you were buying the place. Remember that conversation when you were buying through them?

'It's a delightful property. You can't go wrong.'

'Well, I'm sure you're right, but the price seems high and it's on our upper limit – well, over the top of it really.'

'High? Oh, not at all. Look, I shouldn't be telling you this, but what you have here is really a distress sale, they want to get rid quickly. Money troubles. You'd hardly find a better bargain.'

'It needs so much doing to it.'

'But what potential! Think how it can look when you've settled in and decorated it. Those *delicious* bow windows.'

'And it hasn't got proper drainage.'

'Oh, you've no worries there. Most country properties have septic tanks. They're environment-friendly, you know.'

'And it's a bit damp.'

'Damp? Nonsense. Just unlived in. That's no more than condensation on the ground-floor walls. It's a charming old house but it needs someone to love it. I'm sure you're just the people it's looking for.'

'Well, we do like it, but – '

'Look, don't miss an opportunity like this. You would be kicking yourselves for the rest of your natural.'

'Right. Here is our offer.'

But that was yesterday. Now, when you decide to sell the same property, you recall how good that particular agent was at persuading you to buy, so you decide to retain him as your selling agent. He comes out to discuss price with you.

'Yes, I remember this house. It's not everybody's cup of tea, you know.'

'How do you mean?'

'Well, it may take a little shifting. Depends who's in the market, of course.'

'What about price? Where do you think we ought to be?'

'Tricky to say.'

'150-ish?'

'Lord, no!'

'But it cost us nearly 100 and we've spent a fortune on it.'

'Yes, I remember you paid through the nose rather, but you haven't actually done much to it, have you?'

'We've reroofed it, put in central heating, built a garage, landscaped the garden and everything.'

'Yes, I think some of the quintessential character has been lost.'

'And we've improved the drains.'

'Ah, that's another problem. You're not on proper main drains are you. Why is everyone else in the village connected?'

'Everyone else isn't. Houses on this side of the hill don't have a main sewer in the road.'

'What about that rising damp problem. I see there are still patches showing through your wallpaper.'

'We did put in an electro-osmotic dampcourse.'

'Doesn't help if your footings are designed like that, I'm afraid. It's obviously a perennial problem with this house.'

'Can you sell it for us?'

'Hard to say. Time will tell. I expect you're regretting having rushed into buying this place, aren't you?'

There's no need to be too deeply depressed about this agent's reaction. There may be an element of truth in what he says, but he is also trying to make selling the house look difficult so that when he does, it will look as though he has performed a miracle for you. Furthermore, he hasn't reckoned on your own superlative selling prowess.

Preparing for clients

Before you do anything about finding a good estate agent, you must make sure your house is absolutely ready for potential customers. Some of the preparations are rather long-term, so make sure you give yourself enough time. First impressions are crucial, so your decor must be sound and must appear authentic. That means washing dirt off in some places but leaving it on in others to retain a 'period' look. You should take extra trouble with damp patches, having a pot of emulsion paint in exactly the right colour so that you can slap a quick coat on over the patch just before viewing begins. This is why it is essential not to allow viewing on Sundays – not, as you might have thought, so that you can rest after a week's hard selling, but to repair the cosmetics of the house.

Cracks which suggest movement in the walls should be papered over, but be prepared to hang a bit more paper at a moment's notice in case the crack reopens just before the viewers arrive. More serious defects, like actual holes in the wall or areas where plaster has fallen off, should have pictures hung over them. Try to be subtle – hang pictures over sound areas of wall as well, to balance things up. A single line of etchings, running vertically down a load-bearing wall, could give the game away. Where floors are defective, nail the carpet down firmly using glue as well as tacks. This will prevent any sticky-beak surveyor from trying to lift the edge and peer underneath at the rotting floorboards. Windows which stick and are difficult to open and shut – about 90 per cent of them in most old country houses – should have security locks fitted. You don't need to put these on properly, but as long as they are there, they give the impression that the windows would, otherwise, be openable. In the kitchen, have lots of extra cup-board doors fixed to the wall to give the impression that there is far more cupboard space than anyone would have thought possible. If a viewer tries to open any, just explain that you keep them locked because you store really embarrassing things in them – pathology specimens, sex-aids or whatever. That should help to prevent them from wanting to open any more closed doors in your house.

Most old houses smell nasty. You will be quite used to the variety of odours which waft in from various quarters – manure from the neighbouring farm, mildew from the upstairs landing, the inexplicable rotting-corpse smell from the cellar and a sort of indeterminate tang of slow rot coupled with rodent urine which permeates the whole house. Your visitors, if they are moving out of town, will be unused to such an olfactory cocktail. To put them at their ease, you should have a mouse or gerbil cage in the corner of the kitchen. Of course, you won't actually have mice or gerbils in it, unless you are into that sort of livestock, but having the cage there helps to explain the odour.

Some people go to great lengths to disguise smells. An old trick is to put a coffee bean or two under the grill just before the customers arrive. The fragrant aroma is supposed to give the impression of a welcoming atmosphere. What actually happens is that you forget the grill and, by the time you have answered the door and shown your visitors into the kitchen, flames are pouring out of the grill and a heavy pall of smoke is obscuring the bogus cupboard doors and most of the downstairs as well. Of course, if the house is incorrigibly malodorous, burning toast can create the perfect smoke screen.

The garden must look good too, even if none of the buyers is keen on gardening. If you haven't time to do the weeding, at least mow the grass. You'd be amazed at what a difference that makes. Don't allow husbands/wives to leave half-repaired cars or lawn mowers lying about and don't allow wives/husbands to have any washing hanging on the line, unless it's a Hermes scarf or a single Givenchy knicker. Borders, even if they are choked with weeds, can be prettied up with a scattering of bedding plants like ger- aniums or petunias, but don't create a carpet – just dot them about, so that from a distance they look exotic and tempting to plant enthusiasts. If your soil is poor, buy some expensive potting compost and spread a layer of it on the ground near the house, giving the impression that the natural soil all over the garden is that good.

The punters

The worst part of selling your house is having to show the potential buyers round. From the moment they introduce themselves on your doorstep, when you think, 'this sort of person can't possibly want to live *here*', to the point where they say 'goodbye' and walk to their car backwards like minions leaving a royal presence, you have to be on your guard. They're not walking backwards in deference to you anyway, they're looking at the roof. This first visit is absolutely vital. Muff it and you've lost a sale. Make a success of it and you may see them again. It's always the people you hate on sight who keep coming back and back and back, but customers are customers. Treasure them!

By the way, did the agent ring you to say your first viewers were on the way? They didn't? Well, there you are, that's agents for you, inefficiency all the way. The couple in question are a Mr and Mrs Crettynwood. They live in Chislehurst but have decided to come up here because Mr C is a computer-chip chopper and his firm has moved to Cambridge. He is a senior manager with a degree in physics from some obscure university not a million miles from the M6. His hobbies are computing, IT and collecting antique word-processing software. He thinks Keats are those little knobs which hold sails in place on boats and Milton is a disinfectant. Mrs C is an officer in the Chislehurst flower-arranging society and hopes to start a new branch in this area. She is a cordon bleu cook and thinks all television should be heavily censored. She even picks the stamens and pistils out of the flowers she arranges in case they corrupt innocent bystanders.

When they arrive, you have just finished Hoovering, scrubbing, dusting and polishing. You see their brand-new Audi turning into the drive and rush upstairs to take your apron off and tidy your hair. When the bell rings, what do you do? You wait, that's what you do. They will want to have a good look at the front of the house and, since it's the only bit you have had repointed, better let them see a lot of that but none of the rest of the outside.

After a short interval, go to a downstairs window and try to attract their attention. The front door doesn't work, remember, so you've got to entice them round the side. They stare at you. You grin and point to the left. Finally, they cotton on and start to walk. This gives you the chance to observe them. What is she wearing? Smart suit and no hat would have suggested a sensible type, but Mrs Crettynwood is sporting a Thai silk number with high throat and full-length sleeves, set off by a neat little hat and white gloves. She is seriously underweight. Mr C is in a computerman suit – grey polyester.

'Mr and Mrs Prattwood?' Oh dear. A bad start. You got the name wrong. It is very important not to make that kind of mistake at the beginning, unless you promote them. 'Lady Crettynforth?' would have been fine. They correct you and you invite them in. 'I'm afraid we haven't cleaned or anything, so you'll have to take us as you find us,' you lie, involuntarily rubbing your nose in the hopes that it will stay the same size. 'Where would you like to start?' That is a purely rheotorical question because you know exactly what course the tour is going to take. You merely have to give the impression that it is all very relaxed and random and that they have control.

'Upstairs,' says La Crettynwood. She's not as daft as she looks, but he's dafter. He's talking to himself. Oh no, it isn't that. He's pulled a cordless telephone out of his pocket and is babbling into it about megabytes and thirteenth-generation models.

'Fine,' you say. 'We'll just do the kitchen first, as it's on our way.' As you walk in, remember to stand with your back to the wall, covering the slash in the plaster where the chair fell over last week.

'Your grill's on,' says Mrs C.

'I smell coffee,' says Mr C meaningfully.

'Of course,' you lie. 'I thought I'd get some on the go in case you feel like a cup before you leave.'

'There was one of these split-level things in our last house when we moved in,' says Mrs C.

'Ah good. You'll be familiar with the workings, then.'

'We had it removed.'

'Ah.'

'Water softener?'

'Of course.'

'That would have to go too. De-ionised water is too high in salt for safe drinking.'

'Ah.'

'That's self contradicting, dearest,' Mr C says.

'Don't be ridiculous, Gerald.'

'If it were de-ionised, it wouldn't have any sodium or chloride ions in it.'

'I said *salt*, dear. It must be true – Esther Rantzen says so.'

'There is a cold tap straight from the mains,' you say. 'The local tap water really is delicious. Makes the most perfect tea.'

'May we go upstairs now?'

'By all means. Let's just do the sitting room on our way, shall we?'

But, as soon as your hand touches the door handle, you remember that your spouse was in there yesterday concealing the loud-speaker leads. The carpet is up, revealing worm-eaten boards, there are tools scattered all over the floor and coils of wire hanging in festoons from the curtain rails, which now have cobwebs hanging over their edges.

'Oh my goodness!' you cry, slamming the door shut, 'I nearly forgot the oven. I'll just run you upstairs and leave you there for a moment or two while I clear – er, empty – my oven.'

While they are looking at the bedrooms you sprint downstairs, falling the last five steps, and within seconds you are wrestling with the sitting-room carpet and trying to pull down the wires at the same time. The ears of your spouse, safely ensconced in a comfortable office miles away, are burning furiously but then, so is the grill, which you've left on. At this point you must keep calm and collected. Leave them upstairs for a while. They probably won't notice the cracked windowpane, the Swedish pornography book you think might be hanging out of the bookcase, the strange hole behind the bed in the master bedroom (the one the draught seems to blow through when the wind is in the west) or the wet patch on the *en-suite* bathroom floor which you've stood the laundry basket on. You get the sitting room more or less straight, put on the coffee (for real, this time) and then sprint up just in time to see Mrs C reaching for the laundry basket which hides the wet spot. You leap between her and it and say, 'Lovely view from that window, isn't it?' They go over to look and you glance at the bookcase, noticing with relief that all the bookbacks are uniformly straight. 'You can see Sliding Bumstead church from here,' you add brightly.

'We straightened your books,' says Mrs C. 'I noticed an interesting title, *Climax in Colour*. You take your decor very seriously, evidently.'

'Um, well, yes. Come and see the other bathroom.'

'We've peeped in, thanks.'

'Guest room?'

'Charming. We liked the view from there too. May we see the sitting room now?'

'Of course.'

Hoping it looks all right, you usher them downstairs. They enter. She doesn't notice the hasty repairs you've made, but blenches at the sight of the nude on the wall, a little charcoal drawing of an obese woman picking cockles.

'Rather fine, don't you think? My cousin drew it when he was visiting a naturist beach in north Norfolk. Something a bit Van Gogh about it, don't you think?'

'Shocking!'

'Not quite. Little place called Dingle. Just up the coast from Shocking.'

You hear a mumbled noise, like a litany, coming from Mr C but he's just drivelling into his pocket phone again.

'Look,' you say. 'Why don't I just let you wander on your own? Then you can ask me anything you want.' They do just that and fifteen minutes later, when the coffee is well stewed, they come to ask questions – an excellent sign.

'Schools?'

'A good village school, the head's a poppet. The local comprehensives are reputed to be pretty good too. Rural ones usually are.'

'We need real education. How far is the nearest private school?'

'There's a prep school on the old Volveaux Estate – Hatchback Hall. Several public schools are within an hour's drive: Oundingham and Upple are the nearest, but Cartershed isn't that far away.'

'What about services? Do they empty the dustbins?'

'Roughly once a week,' you say. You don't let on that the rubbish has to be put out on the street if you want it taken away and that you never know which day of the week they're coming until they've been and you've missed them.

'What about trains?'

'Oh yes. Plenty from Cambridge.'

'But that's nearly thirty miles away!'

'Mmm, but less than half an hour on the M11.'

The questions go on for a few minutes more and then the inevitable: 'Have you had any offers?'

Now, here you may have to lie through your teeth.

'We've been flooded with viewers.'

'Well, we are interested and would like to come again for really good look, preferably with our surveyor.'

That is a good sign, and you're in with a chance.

Children

Few objects can be more damning to your potential house sale than children. Viewers' children are as deleterious as one's own. They all have an unerring ability to cause maximum embarrassment to all parties. A family's most personal secrets are always dragged out to view by those innocent little darlings, who show not the slightest recognition of the mayhem they have caused.

Just having one's own children around during viewing triples your chances of losing a sale. If you can get rid of them, at least on the first visit, so much the better, but even out of sight they will leave a trail of discouraging obstacles, each of which will put your clients off, stage by stage, until they end up hating the house and having grave misgivings about you. Show them into the bathroom and, however recently you have checked it, one of the children will have slipped in and left the washbasin with a grimy tidemark and all the towels screwed up on the floor, each with conspicuous dirt stains. In the corridor will be a cricket bat, banana skin, one shoe and a pair of underpants – turned inside out – even though, minutes before, you checked the area and all was spic and span.

Show your visitors into the sitting room and, in spite of having rationed your children to watching nothing but educational programmes on TV and even though they are not there themselves, the TV has mysteriously turned itself on and is tuned to one of the most mindless American cartoon series you have ever seen. The 'absent' children will also have made it to the kitchen before you. There'll be a scattering of crumbs on the floor, mugs on most of the work surfaces, some on their sides, spilt milk and a half-eaten piece of toast, butter-side down, in the doorway.

If you decide to play safe and have your children in tow as you escort the punters round the house, things can be even worse. They tend to make *outré* remarks every five minutes and invariably point out the worst of the defects, not only in their parents' characters, which is mortifying, but also in the house, which is jeopardising to the sale. They do such unpredictable things that whenever they are present one tends to be on edge. Such vibes are picked up by the customer, who assumes that you are ill at ease because you are trying to hide the fact that the house has something dire wrong with it.

If the customers bring their own children – some people have the strange idea that their offspring will take an active interest in where they live – then your problems, and theirs, are compounded. The children will kill concentration first, patience second and goodwill third, so that the viewing will start on the wrong foot and end in fiasco. Recently, a fly I happen to be on speaking terms with was on the wall of this particular old farmhouse when the owners were trying to flog it to some people up from London.

Mother: Mrs Dockland? Do come in. We were expecting you. I'm afraid my husband's at work, so it's just me and, of course, my other man about the house, Justin. He's seven.

Justin: Seven and a half, actually, Mummy.

Dockland: Hullo, Justin. I've got Jocasta in the car. She's almost the same age. Would you like to meet her?

Justin: No!

Mother: Justin! [To Dockland] Do fetch her, I'm sure they'd like to play together.

Justin: On no they wouldn't. She might have a funny-shaped face too.

Dockland: I'll just go and fetch her. [Exit]

Mother: You tactless little bastard, you mustn't say things like that! Ah, here you are then. Hullo, you must be Jocasta.

Jocasta: What's that funny smell? Ugh, it's disgusting.

Mother: Well, isn't this jolly. Now, Justin. You take Jocasta – do you call her Jo?

Dockland: No.

Mother: Oh no, of course not. Er, you and Justin could go and play in the playroom and Mrs Dockland and I can have a nice tour of the house. Won't that be fun?

Justin: You didn't say fun at breakfast.

Mother: The playroom, Justin, please.

Justin: You said some silly cow from –

Mother: Justin! [To Dockland] Let me lead the way. [They go upstairs. The children tag along, eyeing each other but sticking like glue to the parents.]

The children will kill concentration first, patience
second and goodwill third.

Mother: This is the master bedroom.

Jocasta: Ugh. What a horrid colour.

Dockland: It's *lovely*. What a nice combination of pinks. I love the little rug.

Mother: There's a bathroom *en suite* here.

Jocasta: Ooh look, Mummy, they've got a green bath, just like Granny's. You know, the one you said proved Granny Dockland was a Philistine. [They go to another room.]

Mother: This is Justin's playroom. Why don't you two little ones play in here?

Jocasta: No. I want to stay with you, Mummy. I don't like this room. It's horrid and *he's* horrid. Makes me feel sick. [They visit the other bedrooms and bathroom.]

Mother: Well, that's about it for upstairs. Let's go to the ground floor.

Dockland: It says there's a study in the particulars. My husband would work from home quite a lot so, perhaps we could see that.

Mother: Absolutely. It's a darling little room.

Justin: What Daddy calls his licensed cupboard. He keeps his extra drinks in there.

Mother: Extra? Justin, show Mrs Dockland the way, and Justin?

Justin: What?

Mother: Don't open Daddy's cupboard.

Justin: [To Dockland] It's in there. There's just room for this desk and that cupboard. Look. [Goes to open cupboard.]

Mother: Justin. Don't open it . . . NO! [But she's too late. He has opened both doors wide and out falls an avalanche of rugby boots, an empty whisky bottle, several golfballs, a walking stick, hip flask, shooting gloves, old dog bone, binoculars, camera, a potato growing sprouts, a couple of books – the selected writings of William Hazlitt, you notice, and an Anthony Burgess novel – and an avalanche of magazines which include *Practical Gardening*, *Country Life* and something with lots of legs and other protuberances on the cover and called *Up and Coming*.]

Dockland: On my goodness!

Mother: Men! So untidy, don't you think?

Dockland: Well, really. What a mess. Shall I help you pick it all up? [She makes no attempt to bend down.] I wouldn't allow my hus –

Jocasta: That's just like Daddy's private cupboard, isn't it, Mummy? Except Daddy's smells worse.

Justin: I shouldn't touch the wall there Mrs Dockland, the paint's probably still wet.

Dockland: Oh, newly decorated?

Justin : No, Mummy just paints that bit every morning.

Mother: [Angry] Justin! Go to the playroom and take Jocasta. NOW!

Jocasta: I *am* going to be sick. I warned you, Mummy. [Vomits copiously all over the Axminster]

Justin: [Deeply impressed] Wow! Would you like to come and see my electric train set. It's really special. Nobody's seen it except for my bestest friend.

Jocasta: All right. [They go out, taking care not to step in the vomit.]

While they are away together, Mother and Mrs Dockland are able to get down to business and discuss everything about the house, local services and so on. What they don't realise is that the two little darlings have become bored with the special train set and are now dismantling the video before moving to a spot of comparative anatomy.

Building the Hype

So far, we've been rather negative in our approach, assuming that the house will be difficult to shift and that we stand to make a capital loss on the deal. But there are ways in which the price can be enhanced, often far beyond the true value. The basis of these techniques consists of building up the image of the house, inflating it to a larger stature than it really has. Here's how.

Local royalty

Parts of Gloucestershire have become exclusive in recent years because members of the Royal Family have taken to living there – or at least to having mansions there. Try something similar with your own area. When showing customers round, remind them that certain Personages are moving in nearby. You mustn't name names, of course, but you can pretend that you've been sworn to secrecy for security reason.

History

A house which was used or visited by an important figure in history will always be in greater demand. If you can't document your statements, be vague about dates and times but be sure to pick a personality who matches the building. One of Queen Elizabeth's advisers is hardly likely to have lived in a house built in 1725. Priest holes are good selling points. If you haven't got one already, get one built in or explain that there had been one but those vandalous Victorians ripped it out. Victorians can be blamed for most things.

Famous architects and landscapers

Most houses which were built by famous architects are well documented. Unless you have records, it is probably better not to claim that Vanbrugh or Wyatt built your house – well, not in writing anyway. Gardens are another matter. They are much shorter-lived and usually poorly documented, so it is easy to create an entire mythology around the origins of your garden. For instance, Gertrude Jekyll designed about a hundred gardens in Edwardian times, but she is credited with thousands. Any rough field with a few trees in it is a 'Capability Brown' landscape and so on.

Treasure trove

This can be a last desperate bid to bolster flagging prices, but it has been successful with gullible customers. You simply let them find out that there is rumoured to be a crate of gold sovereigns or a medieval gold goblet hidden somewhere about the house. Naturally, you've never been able to find it, but there was this odd parchment plan that was spotted in the attic and has a strange code on it which points to the well in the cellar.

Moving

Removal firms have two purposes.

1 They are secretly hired by furniture manufacturers to destroy as many household effects as possible so that the market for replacements continues to grow.

2 Their furniture vans are designed to block as much traffic as possible. To ensure this they have huge, bulky bodies which spread from one side of the road to the other and engines which are so underpowered that as soon as the van arrives at a 1 in 200 incline, it is forced to slow to crawling pace.

When you know your moving date, you will have to organise a removal firm to come in, pack, stack and convey your things. They will also be required at the other end to unpack the broken pieces. Some weeks before the dreaded day, one of the firm's representatives will call to assess the size of the job. Glancing cursorily round the rooms he will make a note or two and within a few days you will receive a quotation. This is the point at which you wonder whether you still want to move. The quote comes to fractionally less than the best offer you have received for your house. You try another firm. This time the figure is higher. You decide to go with the first quote.

On packing-day morning, you unlock the front door at six-thirty sharp, as instructed by the removal firm. Time creeps by. Nobody comes. You decide to telephone.

'Pockforth Removals. How may I help you?' says the telephone girl. You ask for the rep, who, as luck would have it, is in his office.

'What's happened?' you say. 'We were expecting you at six-thirty.'

'That's right.'

'But it's nearly eleven.'

'Yes.'

'So where are you?'

'Well, here. We're not due at your house until the 24th.'

'Have you got a calendar?'

'Oh my goodness. My men have gone to Runcorn. Runcorn was supposed to have been the 25th.'

'What do we do?'

'Have to be tomorrow. I'm terribly sorry.'

Reorganising your whole move exercises your mind and keeps you busy for hours. Next day they turn up at six-fifteen, two pantechnicons and six men.

'Bit early for you, are we, squire?' asks the foreman.

'Twenty three and three-quarter hours late, actually,' you quip, and then regret it, because you realise that your most precious possessions are going to be in his hands. You try to make amends for your sarcasm by offering coffees all round.

'We'll let you now when we're ready for coffee breaks, squire,' he says, and then, 'Right, lads. Let's be 'aving yer.'

They begin to hurl things into tea chests – porcelain first, then clocks on top and then your heavy bronze figurines on top of them. You notice a clock's winding key fall into the newspaper they are using as packing material.

'Steady!' you shout, 'a key.'

Somebody picks it up and gives it to you. It is unfamiliar. Someone else's. You wonder how many of your own tiny items will go missing. As the day wears on, you realise that they have had five coffee breaks and have actually been sitting down for a longer period than they have been packing. You also notice that your best antiques are being crammed in roughly, wherever they will fit, but cheap, easily replaced items are being handled as if they were Fabergé eggs. At last it's all done and they are off. In store overnight and then to your new house tomorrow.

'See you in Richmond, then, gov,' says the foreman. 'Be about half-past-ten termorrer.'

'Fine,' you say. 'Better just have the phone number of the new place. You know the address?'

'Of course. Rydal Lane. See yer!'

You drive yourself to Richmond and camp in your new house overnight. Needless to say, they don't turn up, but at eleven there's a phone call.

'Can't find Rydal Lane, boss. We've tried everywhere. Post office say they don't know it either.'

'Where exactly are you?'

'Richmond, like.'

'What, in the centre?'

'More or less.'

'Well, just look for Kew Road. We're between Kew Gardens and Richmond.'

'Queue Gardens? Whereabouts is that, then?'

'Just round the corner from Richmond Park. Have a look in your *A–Z*.'

'I don't think there is an *A–Z* for Yorkshire, squire – that's more yer Greater London.'

'What? I do *not* believe it. You've gone to Richmond, Yorks.?'

'Yeah. Richmond, like. That's where you said to go.'

'Have you the faintest inkling of how far you are from London?'

Will the furniture vans ever find Richmond, Surrey? Will you be happy now you are back in the City or will the first fog have you hankering for those primrose-studded lanes again? If you ever do yearn for rusticity again, get straight on to a tube and go to Piccadilly Circus – it's about as far as you can get from the country – and wait there until the feeling has passed.